The Paradise Co-ordinates

To the memory of my
late father and mother,
Norman and Peggy Pollard,
and to my late sister Angela

John R. Pollard

The Paradise Co-ordinates
The Enigma
of Rennes-le-Château

edited and with additional material
by Peter Cowlam

and with a foreword by Charles Camp

Arcatrans Inc Ltd

Published in 2002 by Arcatrans Inc Ltd,
Hale Nook House, Out Rawcliffe,
Preston, PR3 6ST

email arcatrans@aol.com

Copyright © 2002, John R. Pollard, Peter Cowlam

The right of John R. Pollard and Peter Cowlam to be identified as the authors of this work has been asserted herein in accordance with the Copyright, Designs and Patents Act 1988.

All rights reserved. This book is sold subject to the condition that it shall not, by way of trade or otherwise, be lent, resold, hired out or otherwise circulated without the publisher's prior consent in any form of binding or cover other than that in which it is published and without a similar condition including this condition being imposed on the subsequent purchaser.

British Library Cataloguing in Publication Data
A catalogue record for this book is available from the British Library.

ISBN 0-9541881-0-1

Printed and bound in Great Britain
by Colin Cross Printers, Garstang, Lancs.

On each side an Imperial City stood,
With Towers and Temples proudly elevate
On seven small Hills, with Palaces adorn'd,
Porches and Theatres, Baths, Aqueducts,
Statues and Trophies, and Triumphal Arcs,
Gardens and Groves presented to his eyes,
Above the heighth of Mountains interpos'd.
By what strange Parallax or Optic skill
Of vision multiplied through air, or glass
Of Telescope, were curious to inquire...

Milton, *Paradise Regained*, Book IV

Contents

Acknowledgements	vii
Foreword	x
Introduction	xi
1 Early history	1
2 The Cathars and the Templars	7
3 Bérenger Saunière	12
4 The clues	15
5 Symphonie pastorale	22
6 Brief survey of the Christian controversy	26
7 Earthly powers	32
8 Voices in the wilderness	37
9 'Peace 681'	44
10 Venus and the winter solstice	48
11 Hermeneutics	54
12 Blue apples	64
13 Was Jerusalem builded here	68
14 Relics and remnants	73
15 Last visit to Rennes-le-Château	79
16 Closing steps	87
Afterword	92
Appendix, Diagrams, Maps, Prints and Astronomy	95
	to 106
Sources	107
Château d'Arques	108
The Author in Rennes-le-Château	109

Acknowledgements

Although my interest in Rennes-le-Château finds its first seeds back in the 1960s, I have never at any time since had the luxury of regular and extended trips to that magical place. That has meant I have had to weave together the two main strands of my theory little by little, and as opportunity allowed. I can scarcely ignore the industry that Rennes-le-Château has become over those thirty to forty years, and the enormous number of books the subject has spawned (and even these days websites!). I make no apology for adding a book and web links of my own, in what I am sure is new light on this mystery. My interpretation of the clues to it, and of the very site itself, so far as I can tell have no precedent in all the printed matter to date.

Of those many books I mention, some undoubtedly offer both the general reader and researchers like myself a great deal of useful information, and what follows is a list of those I would like to single out as having been of particular value to me. These are:

The Holy Blood and the Holy Grail, jointly authored by Michael Baigent, Richard Leigh and Henry Lincoln. *The Holy Place*, by Henry Lincoln. *The Holy Grail Revealed*, by Patricia and Lionel Fanthorpe. *The Treasure Seeker's Treasury*, by Roy Norvill. *Signé: Rose Croix*, by Gérard de Sède. Other books, not specifically about Rennes-le-Château, but which were critical to my inquiries, are as follows:

Carta's Historical Atlas of Jerusalem, by Dan Bahat. *The Dead Sea Scrolls Deception*, by Michael Baigent and Richard Leigh. *The Throne of David*, by A. G. Hebert. *Jesus: The Evidence*, by Ian Wilson. *An Illustrated Encyclopaedia of Traditional Symbols*, by J. C. Cooper. *The Round Art*, by A. T. Mann. *Longitude*, by Dava Sobel. *A History of Europe*, by J. M. Roberts.

I would also like to thank New Directions Publishing Corporation, Publishers Penguin UK, for permission to quote from J. L. Borges's short story 'Tlön, Uqbar, Orbis Tertius', published in the collection *Labyrinths* (Penguin, 1986), in a translation by James E. Irby. Thanks also to my illustrator, Richard Unthank, whose highly sophisticated computer enhancement techniques graphically point up my exposition of particular geometric relationships, notably lines and angles underpinning well known parchment evidence, as well as those traceable in Poussin's *Shepherds of Arcadia* and Teniers' depiction of St Anthony and St Paul.

I am indebted too to the following for the reproduction or adaptation of key figures, paintings or illustrations: A. T. Mann, for his illustration showing the relationship between the ecliptic and equator (see my Figure 1), published in his *The Round Art* (Dragon's World Ltd, 1979); the Louvre in Paris, for Poussin's *Shepherds of Arcadia* (my Figure 2); Tatiana Kletzky-Pradere, for the map of Rennes-le-Château (my Figure 4); Carta, The Israel Map and Publishing Company Ltd, Jerusalem, for the map of Jerusalem in the Crusader period (my Figure 5); and to the Whipple Museum of the History of Science, Cambridge University, for the illustration of a paper horary quadrant by Henry Sutton (my Figure 7).

My personal thanks go to Charles Camp, who in the early days of the 1980s financed Elaine Swann's first expedition to Rennes-le-Château. My time at that period was extremely limited, and it was Elaine who was able to provide sound advice as to the geography of the gardens and layout of the village. Ever since then, Charles has been a constant source of encouragement, and as keen as I to see the mystery solved.

In my search and endeavour over all these years, somehow crammed into a hectic life in the world of container management and the shipping industry, Hazel Stokes, a close and long-term friend, has been ever willing to provide a sounding post for some of the thoughts and ideas I tossed around when my book was merely a growing wodge of notes. Farooq Hasan, an old friend from my shipping days, also inspired me to finish the book.

My most special thanks go to Jane Duckett, who although she came to the project late (in 2001), was instrumental in cementing the final analysis, through her sharp observations of the region's flora, and a fresh interpretation of many of the mystery's key words, all evidently lost on previous researchers.

Thanks too to Mike Eastman for his translation from de Sède, which appears in Chapter 12, and special thanks to my editor Peter Cowlam, for his enormous energy and sheer literary verve.

Inevitably, chasing down the copyright holders of some source material proved extremely difficult, despite my best efforts. Should anybody be of the opinion that anything appearing in these pages has been reproduced without the appropriate authority, apologies are due, and an invitation to contact the publisher.

Foreword

The Paradise Co-ordinates reads less like a treasure hunt and more as a feat of detection, where the sleuth has devoted great chunks of his life to the abiding riddle of Rennes-le-Château, that settlement in south west France where Saunière, a nineteenth-century priest, opened a Pandora's box, its mysterious contents proving a puzzle to inquisitive minds ever since.

Now at last John R. Pollard, a friend and colleague of mine over many years, has shown I think once and for all what all its elements add up to, and all its paraphernalia. Religious sects, conquering empires, a Renaissance painter, a long train of mythological symbols, almost impossibly difficult codes and encryptions – added to which we must now not overlook Saunière's paradise on earth, and all the ancient associations that implies.

Yet the author's revelatory text is only one of his book's virtues, for not only does he bring to it a new historical perspective – he gives us a sprinkling of poetry too. Naturally enough, John R. Pollard unravels his quest against the backdrop of the Corbières countryside, douched in the scent of thyme, and with a spectacular surrounding landscape as rich for its vineyards as it is rugged for its barren hillsides, where we as readers can almost feel the searing heat of summer or the scything winds of winter.

The Paradise Co-ordinates encapsulates an image of the past and sets it in context with the simpler hopes and yearnings people continue to experience here in our post-industrial age. In the end it's a book that not only unveils a long-standing secret, it probes to the heart of our human will, laying bare the power as individuals all of us crave, and that Saunière alone among his peers was able to grasp. That was the power of choice.

Charles E. Camp, Suffolk, 2001

Introduction

Much has already been written on the subject of Rennes-le-Château, a village in the rolling countryside of south west France. This is because many still believe in its buried treasure, as I do too. I also believe that I alone have discovered how to find it.

The dramas and sheer sense of arcane mystery veiling this tiny settlement's secret hoard have drawn many of my predecessors into heroic and often ingenious attempts to unravel its enigmas. Prime among these is Bérenger Saunière, who in 1885 arrived in Rennes-le-Château as its church's new curate. When he began his new career, it was in a much impoverished state, but with the discoveries he soon made he came to enjoy enormous and fabulous wealth, which to the people around him was as baffling as it was miraculous. It is the question as to precisely how he uncovered these riches that has stimulated so much subsequent interest, in my case to the point of working out – just as Saunière had done – the precise location of that hoard.

Rennes-le-Château is in the Languedoc region. This is a part of southern France whose long and eventful history has encompassed the treasures of Jerusalem and Rome, the Franks, the Merovingians, the Carolingians, the Cathars and the Knights Templar. That history has often been turbulent. Even so, it remains a small village whose environs are relatively untouched, a remote haven in a spectacular setting, blissfully detached from all our familiar pressures of modern urban living.

I first came into the region by road in 1964, with my parents and my sister, who was fluent in French – which made it her job to translate and to do all our talking. I was then nineteen, and my job was to drive. That meant a journey in the family car of some 3,000 kilometres to the Pyrenees and back – a trip that for me was destined to be just the first of many steps in a lifelong voyage of discovery. I can recall it vividly. The hot sticky macadam on the roadways threw up its mirages. Our car, with a younger, racier me at the wheel, sped from one hairpin bend to the next, on roads and in a countryside not yet discovered by the tourist hordes. We had stopped off at places such as Quillan, Elne, and Collioure, which is considered by many the jewel of the Mediterranean. In the mountains were endless idyllic spots, with the sun in its perfect blue heaven, and a serenade of purling streams. I remember too in the small towns or villages how we took our meals with the locals, sometimes in the cool of their cafés, on other occasions outside in the shade of the plane trees.

I longed to return, and even then could contemplate return. Fired by that, I naturally developed an interest in the region's history. Why, for example, were there so many castles? These – fantastic, gaunt constructions, clinging to the mountainsides – dated from the thirteenth century and even before, and in the mid-1960s remained largely untouched by tourism. Historically too the region had matured in its production of foodstuffs and wine, with its goat and sheep cheeses, peach harvests, and perhaps most important of all its famous Corbières vineyards.

My subsequent explorations took place firstly during the mid-60s to early 1970s, then in the mid-80s, then in 1999, the last days of the twentieth century. I began to learn how the wild foothills of the eastern Pyrenees had been at the forefront of so many power struggles, particularly during the Albigensian crusade. Great wealth and power had been bestowed on individual counts and barons from the houses of Toulouse, Béziers and Carcassonne. The whole area was more or less a series of princedoms in its own right, with trading and cultural ties through Spain, Arabia and the eastern Mediterranean.

That collision of cultures is evident in the various architectural styles adorning the towns and villages. There is a Phoenician tower in Collioure which is used as a church. There are bastide villages (fortified settlements typically founded in south western France in the Middle Ages), and castles with crypts. One finds villages on hilltops, and religious centres such as Cordes are perched on dizzy ridges. Castles can be enormous, like the one at Carcassonne, while others are forbidding and isolated, built precipitously into clifftop ridges. One of the most famous among these is Montségur – a mountain retreat topping a buttress of rock. Inevitably one asks, what provoked these constructions in such unlikely places, where provisions – most importantly water – must have been hard to come by? How could such places sustain a living population through so many years, in particular through the years of conflict?

Well, I have since come to learn a very great deal about the hills of Aude, in the villages of Rennes-le-Château, Rennes-les-Bains, Couiza and Arques. It's a tapestry of knowledge I find myself ever willing to reconstruct, whose first sparkle of wealth is bound up with its early history, and whose final thread is the golden one of Saunière's secret hoard – to which I will lead you. In passing perhaps also we should speculate, as others have done before me, not only on what that treasure is exactly, but who it was that put it there. A case can be made for any of the following – the Romans, the Visigoths, the Franks or the Carolingians, the Knights Templar, or even an heretical Christian sect such as the Cathars.

Sea Holly.

1 Early history

Rennes-le-Château lies south of the walled city of Carcassonne in the Aude *département* of France, an area that borders the Corbières wine country, close to the western Mediterranean. It is partly ruined, is situated on a hilltop, and commands extensive views. It and the surrounding country were important politically from the earliest Roman times, the Romans having a presence in Rennes-les-Bains, which is a spa village built in a ravine about two to three kilometres away.

By the third century BCE Rome had completed its conquest of Italy, had emerged as a world power, and now disputed with Carthage for control of the western Mediterranean. At that time Carthage was a major commercial entity, and the battles that followed were known as the Punic Wars. Two military giants were among the respective leaders – Hannibal, who for twenty years commanded the Carthaginians, and the Roman commander Scipio, who in 200 defeated him. This, as a victory, was seen as of such magnitude that it stimulated Rome to further conquest, which in turn brought further acquisitions. Its next target was the entire Mediterranean area, where to the east Syria, Macedonia, Greece and Egypt were all defeated.

On the back of these triumphs the Romans reorganised their conquered peoples into provinces, which they controlled through the appointment of governors. Governors wielded absolute power over all non-Roman citizens, and were supported by stationed troops. In Rome itself, paradoxically, most citizens suffered rather than profited from enterprise abroad. Farmers weren't able to compete economically with their new counterparts in the provinces, and it was soon the case that in terms of living standards, an all too obvious gap existed between the common people and the aristocracy. At the heart of the problem was the Roman economy, which being built on slavery was highly rewarding for some but for most others was a disaster. The casualties were placated initially through the purchase of necessities and entertainments, which Roman wealth was well able to muster. Much of this wealth was in the form of gold coins, struck in various mints, one of which was at Arles, not that far east of Rennes-le-Château. Yet, despite that wealth and its purchasing power, resentment increased. Civil wars were inevitable, and the revolution that followed signalled the transition of Rome from republic to empire.

The last stages of the civil wars saw the careers of Pompey, Cicero and Julius Caesar, Caesar taking full power over Rome as dictator. He was assassinated in 44 BCE, and was followed by the triumvirs – Mark Antony, Lepidus and Caesar's nephew Octavian. Octavian waged war against Antony in northern Africa, and having defeated him was crowned as Rome's first emperor. Other emperors followed, among them Trajan, Hadrian, Antoninus Pius and Marcus Aurelius – all of whom were loved. But there were cruel emperors also, such as Caligula and Nero – by contrast both of these were hated.

It was during the rule of Tiberius (14-37 CE) that Christ was crucified, after which Christians were at best tolerated, at worst tortured or killed. Judaism also suffered, and in 70 CE Jerusalem was sacked, the Romans making off with much of its temple treasure. Changed attitudes towards religion came about under the reign of Constantine I (312-337), one of whose early acts was an edict of toleration for all creeds, with Christianity becoming the empire's official religion from about 320. By now however the empire's best days had gone, and the last of Constantine's line, Theodosius I, was also the last to rule over a unified empire. The west suffered repeated invasions and grew weak compared with the east, where spices and other exports were a continuing source of wealth. Theodosius died in 395, at which point Rome split into two – into its eastern and western empires – a division that had a direct bearing on the events, wealth and fortune surrounding Rennes-le-Château.

The western empire suffered badly in 410, when Rome was sacked by the Visigoths. These were a wandering Germanic people who had separated from the Ostrogoths in the previous century. With that split the Visigoths embarked on persistent raids into Roman territories, and in the process established their own kingdoms in Gaul and Spain. In 378 they engaged with Valens, the then Roman emperor, on the plains outside Adrianople – an event that saw the defeat of Roman infantry at the hands of barbarian horsemen. This represented only the start of major Germanic progress into Roman territory.

The Visigoths continued to wander in search of new horizons. In 382 Theodosius, who had succeeded Valens, settled them as federates in Moesia, with land and the job of defending the frontier. They remained here, converts to Arian Christianity, until 395, then moved south to Greece, then on to Italy. This was under the leadership of Alaric, who also led them to the sack of Rome in 410. When Alaric died Ataulphus took over, and settled them first in southern Gaul, then later in Spain (in 415). In 418 they acted again as federates to Rome, this time in the province of Aquitania Secunda, an area of modern-day France between the Garonne and Loire rivers. Their chieftain Wallia died soon after this and was succeeded by Theodoric I. Theodoric remained their ruler until his own death in 451, suffered in his fight against Attila during the battle of the Catalaunian Plains.

Despite these losses the Visigoths continued to test the bounds of their territory, which – though they remained federates until 475 – was often at the empire's expense. Theodoric's son Euric declared himself king while his Gallic kingdom, whose capital was Toulouse, achieved its greatest extent, stretching from the Loire to the Pyrenees and to the lower reaches of the Rhône. It also included much of Spain. In the following year the fall of Rome was complete, with the German chieftain Odoacer deposing the west's last Roman emperor, Romulus Augustulus, while the wealthier, stronger east continued as the Byzantine empire throughout the Middle Ages.

Euric was succeeded by his son Alaric II, who was defeated and killed in 507 by Clovis and the Franks. This was at the battle of Vouillé, near Poitiers. As a result the Visigoths lost – apart from Septimania – all their possessions in Gaul, Septimania being a ribbon of land extending along the coast from the Pyrenees to the Rhône, with Narbonne as its capital. The Franks, a Germanic-speaking people, were never able to win this from them, though had also been busy invading the western Roman empire. They came to dominate what is today northern France, Belgium and western Germany, and the name

France is derived from the word Frank.

In the third century the Franks were divided into three distinct groups – the Salians, Ripuarians and Hessians. Although related to one other by virtue of language and custom, politically they remained independent. In the middle of the third century they all made unsuccessful attempts at expansion westward into Gaul. In the middle of the fourth century they tried it again, this time with better luck, since in 358 Rome abandoned the area between the Meuse and Scheldt rivers (now in Belgium) to the Salians. In the course of these struggles the Franks like the Visigoths would sometimes ally themselves to the Romans in defence of their frontier.

The Vandals also pressed their case, launching their own invasion of Gaul in 406, and in the wake of that the Franks took advantage of the Romans' overstretched defences. They strengthened their grip on what is now Belgium, took control of the lands west of the middle Rhine, and edged into what today is north eastern France.

In around 482 Childeric was succeeded by his son Clovis I as ruler of the Salian Franks of Tournai. Clovis took advantage of the empire's disintegration, and having united the Franks led them in a series of campaigns that established northern Gaul to his rule. He drove on south, overcoming the Visigoths, and thereafter adopted Catholicism, the conversion to orthodox Christianity serving as one more means by which the Franks united themselves as a people. When Clovis died in 511, his realm was divided among his four sons. Despite competition between them, the brothers succeeded in enlarging Frankish rule over Thuringia (in approximately 531) and Burgundy (in 534). They won influence but not possession over Septimania, over Bavaria, and over the Saxon lands to the north. By 558 Chlotar I was the sole surviving brother, and with that the Frankish realm was united once more, until his death in 561, when the realm was again divided – and again there was strife. This saw Chilperic and his wife Fredegund, in the north west of Gaul, pitted against Sigebert with his wife Brunhilda, in the north east.

Dynastic conflicts, and external pressures exerted by neighbouring peoples – Bretons and Gascons in the west, Lombards in the south east, Avars in the east – brought about a reorganisation of the Frankish kingdoms. Eastern regions were subsumed into the kingdom of

Austrasia, whose capital was Metz. Neustria emerged in the west, its capital first at Soissons, then later at Paris. South saw the enlarged kingdom of Burgundy, with its capital at Chalon-sur-Saône. Frankish unity didn't return again until 613, when Chlotar II, the king of Neustria, inherited the other two kingdoms – though when Chlotar's son Dagobert died in 639 the realm was again split. However, by that time, the kings of the two regions – which on the one hand were Neustria and Burgundy, on the other Austrasia – had given up much of their power to household officials known as mayors of the palace. Mayors of the palace had positioned themselves prominently *vis-à-vis* the later dynasty of Frankish kings, known as the Merovingians – who by now were really puppet kings – and who were putty in their hands, enthroned or deposed at will.

One of the later Merovingians was the king of Austrasia, Dagobert II, or St Dagobert, whose name plays a central role in the mystery of Rennes-le-Château's hidden treasure. Dagobert was born circa 650 and died on 23rd December 679, near Stenay, Lorraine. His feast day is also 23rd December, one day after the winter solstice. He was the son of Sigebert III, whose death in 656 resulted in Dagobert's dispatch to an Irish monastery, an event that saw his throne assumed by Childebert the Adopted, himself son to an Austrasian mayor of the palace. Inevitably these impostors did suffer a temporary downfall, at which point Dagobert's cousin Chlotar III secured the Austrasian throne for Childeric II, in 662. When Childeric was assassinated in 675 Dagobert was traced, and restored to the throne in the following year. It was his murder three years after this that led to the unity of all Frankish lands under Theodoric III.

Childeric III, the last Merovingian, was deposed by Pepin III the Short in 750, one in a line of Austrasian mayors of the palace. It was he who finally usurped the throne and established the Carolingian dynasty. The Carolingian Charlemagne, or Charles the Great, who reigned 768-814, restored the western Roman empire in co-operation with the papacy, so spreading Christianity into central and northern Germany, but by the middle of the ninth century his empire too had disintegrated.

§

One very influential book on the mysteries surrounding Rennes-le-Château, published in the early 1980s, is *The Holy Blood and the Holy Grail*, co-authored by Michael Baigent, Richard Leigh and Henry Lincoln. It reads as an interesting amalgam of hypothesis, speculation and scholarly research, where a good deal of documentary evidence is adduced in support of the authors' various theses. One of these theses is the historical presence of an organisation known as the Priory of Sion, which the book demonstrates as one powerfully attached to the inception of the Knights Templar. The Knights Templar were a religious military order of knighthood founded in the early years of the kingdom of Jerusalem, when Christian crusaders controlled few strongholds in the Holy Land, and pilgrims to the holy places were often at the mercy of marauding Muslim bands. Baigent, Leigh and Lincoln introduce a strong case for the continued existence of the Priory of Sion, long after the disappearance of the Templars. They offer as an important focus of their argument the proposition that this organisation is still active today. Why should that be?

The Priory's aim, apparently, is the reinstatement of the Merovingians to the French throne, even at this remove from Dagobert, whose lineage, by 711, had been driven into hiding in the Razès, the region of Rennes-le-Château. Intriguingly the name Dagobert is, as we shall see, inextricably linked to the treasures of Rennes-le-Château, riches which Saunière (in the capacity of Catholic priest) uncovered, and whose footsteps I propose to trace. Whether or not this will ultimately lead to the Priory of Sion – a sort of secret Masonic society – I wouldn't at this stage care to speculate. It does however plunge us into the disputes of Saunière's creed, prime among which was the problem posed by the Cathars.

2 The Cathars and the Templars

The small church in Rennes-le-Château was constructed in the tenth or eleventh century, and after that a tiny settlement sprang up around it on its hilltop. A few hundred years later the Cathar church rose to prominence, and briefly surpassed the rule of Rome.

The Cathars were an heretical Christian sect that flourished in western Europe in the twelfth and thirteenth centuries. Central to their creed was a neo-Manichaean dualism, which saw the universe as resting on two principles – one good, one evil. According to them, the material world was evil.

Manichaeanism was a religious movement founded in third-century Persia by a man called Mani. Mani was born in southern Babylonia, which today is Iraq, and preached throughout the Persian empire. Essentially Manichaeanism was a brand of Gnosticism, which offered salvation through knowledge of spiritual truth. It taught that life was painful and evil, and that the soul, akin to the nature of God, had fallen into the evil world of matter, and therefore must be saved. The saving was done by the spirit, or intelligence, which was all bound up with the self. To know one's self was to recover one's true self. One's true self had been previously clouded by ignorance, a state brought about through co-habitation with the body, which was part of the material world, and therefore with matter, and therefore with evil. To know one's self was to share in the nature of God, and belong to a transcendent world.

Gaining this knowledge ensured that the enlightened person understood the issues of spirit versus matter, despite the fact of his or her subjection to the material universe. It followed therefore that knowledge was salvation, that our human path was a path of fallen souls, and that the right human path was of souls temporarily ensnared by evil – but then liberated by spirit. In wider, cosmic terms, the three evolutionary stages overarching all of this were a past where two opposed substances had separated – spirit and matter, good and evil, light and darkness – a middle period (the present) where the two substances had become mixed – and a future where the original duality would reform. A return to paradise was promised to the souls of righteous persons, and for those who persisted in the things of the flesh, who weren't righteous persons, there could only ever be rebirth (which, as an obvious parallel with Buddhism, a religion much older than Christianity, is not so radical a concept). Much though that ethos was absorbed into Cathar discipline and structure, it was only a fraction of the faithful who followed its strict ascetic or monastic life. These were termed the elect. The elect were supported by their hearers with works and alms.

Manichaeanism spread rapidly west into the Roman empire. It moved across northern Africa, reaching Rome in the early fourth century. The fourth century witnessed the height of its expansion, with churches in southern Gaul and Spain. Predictably it suffered attack, at the hands of both the Christian church and the Roman state, and disappeared from western Europe almost entirely by the end of the fifth century – though didn't disappear from the eastern empire till the sixth. That said, its influence never entirely receded: in the first half of the eleventh century isolated groups of heretics whose espoused views were similar to those of the Manichaeans appeared in western Germany, Flanders and northern Italy. One further example in the twelfth century was that of the Bogomil church, one of whose tenets was a denial of the divine birth of Christ and of the validity of sacraments and ceremonies. It might also be added that there were Bogomil missionaries at work in the west when western dualists were returning from the second crusade (1147-49), which campaign had been a failure.

The Cathars were an organised church from the 1140s, complete with hierarchy, a liturgy, and a system of doctrine. In about 1149 their first bishop established himself in the north of France. A few years later he had colleagues at Albi in southern France – from which the Albigensian crusade derives its name – and at Lombardy. Their status was confirmed and the prestige of the Cathars was uplifted in 1167 when the Bogomil bishop Nicetas paid a visit. In the following years there were more Cathar bishops, and at the turn of the century there were eleven bishoprics in total. One of these was in the north of France. Four were in the south. Six were in Italy.

Although various groups emphasised a different range of doctrines, all were agreed that matter was evil. Man, though enmeshed in an evil world, was not indigenous to it, and his aim was to free his spirit – which in its nature was good. His ultimate aim was communion with God. To this end there were dietary and carnal rules, which included the total prohibition of meat, and of sexual intercourse. In fact renunciation of the world was an imperative. This made the Cathar church a church of the elect, though paradoxically in France and northern Italy the movement was admired by ordinary people. Its success was due to its division of the faithful into two bodies – the so-called 'perfect', and the 'believers'. The 'perfect' were set apart by a ceremony of initiation, called the consolamentum, and devoted themselves to contemplation and the highest moral standards (which the 'believers' weren't expected to attain).

Cathar doctrine led to a reinterpretation of the Bible as largely mythology. The Old Testament was viewed with scepticism, and the incarnation was rejected. Instead Jesus was an angel, whose human sufferings and death were an illusion. The Cathars were also critical of the Catholic church, whose worldliness had mired it in corruption. Cathar doctrine therefore questioned the very basis of orthodox Christianity, and stood to undermine the political institutions of Christendom. Perhaps not surprisingly church and state eventually united against them. Pope Innocent III tried to persuade Raymond VI to help him put down the heresy, though Raymond, who was count of Toulouse from 1194, was inclined to tolerate Catharism in the Languedoc. However, he did in 1209 join what was known as the Albigensian crusade, the year in which Simon de Montfort arrived as one of its leaders. Montfort conquered Béziers and Carcassonne, and these became lands he governed. When most of the crusaders left, he found himself with large territories still to conquer. In 1213, after he won the battle of Muret, he appropriated Raymond's lands – thereafter styling himself not only count of Toulouse, but viscount of Béziers and Carcassonne, and duke of Narbonne. Raymond – perhaps ever an optimist – didn't accept defeat, and in September 1217 occupied

Toulouse. Montfort was killed, and his son Amaury abandoned the crusade, ceding the Montfort lands in southern France to King Louis VIII.

Albigensian theologians and ascetics, known in the south of France as *bons hommes* or *bons chrétiens*, were not that great in number. Few as they were, the common people formed an attachment to them, powerfully drawn to their antisacerdotal preaching and naturally impressed at the strength of their moral position. After much bloodshed, the crusade against them ended. This was in 1229, with the Treaty of Paris. Though that did destroy the independence of the princes in the south, it didn't eliminate the heresy, which persisted until the Inquisition, in the thirteenth and fourteenth centuries (it was the Inquisition which did crush it in the end). In 1244 the great fortress of Montségur, a stronghold of the 'perfect', was besieged. By this time the Cathars were extremely wealthy, and Montségur was a repository of significant treasures. Somehow during the siege a way out was found and all such treasure was secretly removed – perhaps to Rennes-le-Château, though no one knows precisely where. Eventually the fortress was captured and destroyed, and the Cathars went underground. A great many French Cathars fled to Italy, where persecution was less systematic – however by the 1270s its hierarchy had disappeared, as had its treasure.

The Cathars were not unconnected with the Knights Templar. These as we have seen were a religious military order whose existence came about during the crusades, when the crusaders had only few footholds in the Holy Land. In 1119 or early 1120, Hugues de Payens and eight or nine French knights decided to offer pilgrims into the Holy Land protection from marauding Muslim bands. To that end they formed a religious community, with the king of Jerusalem, Baldwin II, assigning them quarters in the royal palace. These quarters were where formerly the Jewish Temple had been (all but destroyed by the Romans in 70 CE), and from this the Templars got their name.

The Temple established links with the Cathars, especially those in the Languedoc. Wealthy Cathar landowners donated land to the Templars, and Bertrand de Blanchefort, the order's fourth grand master, was himself of a Cathar family.

There were four Templar classes: knights, sergeants, chaplains and servants. The white surcoat marked with a red cross – the Templars' distinctive regalia – was worn only by the knights. The entire Templar order was headed by a grand master, with each temple or subsidiary ruled by a commander.

After commencing work in the Holy Land, the order rapidly increased in number (in part due to the propaganda purveyed by St Bernard of Clairvaux, who wrote their rule of life), and until 1139 the Templar vow of obedience was to the patriarch of Jerusalem. Pope Innocent II changed this, and placed the Templars directly under the pope's authority. Effectively this released the Templars from episcopal jurisdiction, and thereafter their activities diversified. They became important defensively to the Christian crusader states of the Holy Land, and in their heyday numbered approximately 20,000 knights.

They acquired vast wealth, and by the middle of the twelfth century owned property in western Europe, the Mediterranean and the Holy Land itself. Their power and military might eased the transportation of bullion through Europe and the Holy Land, and reached a point of organisational efficiency by which the Templars found themselves bankers to kings (among others).

Their end was signalled in 1291 when Acre fell to the Muslims. Acre was the last crusader stronghold in the Holy Land, and with its loss so apparently the Templars' *raison d'être* also disappeared. By 1304 there were rumours in circulation that the Templars were guilty of blasphemies and irreligious practices. On 13th October 1307 King Philip IV the Fair of France had every Templar in France arrested. All their property in France was sequestered. Why Philip did this is unclear. Perhaps he feared Templar power, or since he was short of funds himself perhaps this was mere opportunism. In any event, he accused the Templars of heresy and urged Pope Clement V to act also. In November 1307 the pope ordered the arrest of Templars in every country, and on 22nd March 1312 he suppressed their order. A great many Templars were executed or imprisoned, and in 1314 Jacques de Molay – the order's last grand master – was burned at the stake.

3 Bérenger Saunière

First intimation that treasure was at some point secreted at Rennes-le-Château occurred during the seventeenth century, when a shepherd called Ignace Paris went looking for a lost sheep. Ignace stumbled on the entrance to a cave, and went inside to look. He found himself in a crypt. The crypt was littered with coffers, under the dead gaze of several skeletons. Amazingly the coffers were filled with gold coins. Naturally Ignace helped himself, and with his pockets full of gold returned to his village, where he was quizzed. When he refused to tell anyone where the vault was, he was accused of theft and executed.

Much later, in 1885, the church of Rennes-le-Château received a new curate – Bérenger Saunière, who fared a good deal better than Ignace. Initially Saunière was taken in and looked after by a family more impoverished than he. Their name was Denarnaud. Somehow Saunière was granted church permission to move the Denarnaud family into the presbytery, and he arranged also for Marie – the Denarnaud daughter, still then a teenager – to help him run the church. Thereafter he and Marie became lifelong companions.

In 1891 Saunière raised funds to carry out restoration work to the church, in the course of which it was found that the altar pillars were hollow. Inside one pillar were four or five sealed wooden rolls, one of which contained a parchment. This parchment bore an inscription, its text a mix of French and Latin, which at first glance appeared to be a passage from the Gospels.

The mayor got to hear of it and was soon asking Saunière all about it. Satisfied that the mayor would never on his own interpret the text, Saunière showed it him, and offered the view that the parchments were to do with the Revolution, but were without real value. That temporarily kept the mayor quiet, though Saunière called a halt to his restoration project.

It was in February 1892 that it's believed Saunière went to Paris. Here he sought the help of church paleographers, who examined the parchment text. At this time Saunière also made a few social calls – notably on Emma Calvé, world-famous opera star and friend to Claude Debussy. He and Emma entered a relationship that was destined to endure. Probably as a result of the paleographers' findings, Saunière next headed off to the Louvre, where he acquired a copy of Poussin's *Shepherds of Arcadia*. Poussin was a Renaissance painter, born near Paris in 1594, and who died in Rome in 1665, where he had spent most of his working life. He is known today principally for his scenes from the Bible and from Greco-Roman antiquity, of which *Shepherds of Arcadia* might be said to be an example.

With his print and his paleographers' report, Saunière returned to Rennes-le-Château, having assembled sufficient information to locate whatever treasure was hidden in or around or beneath his church. Evidently one of the parchments yielded a measurement from the church altar to a position outside called the 'castle'. The documents also drew attention to a specific tomb in the churchyard – that of Marie de Nègri D'Ablès, Dame d'Hautpoul de Blanchefort – whose grave- and headstone bore slightly eccentric inscriptions. These turned out to provide a key to the encrypted text of his parchments, which Saunière was now able to decode. When he and Marie dug, it was at the entrance to a vault, whose treasures were intact.

Inevitably Saunière may have sold certain pieces, and thereby amassed his fortune. Whatever was the case, he returned to his restoration work, now conceiving it on a far larger scale than before. The presbytery was repaired and a new wall put up round the churchyard. New works included a summer house, a rock garden, fountains. The five-kilometre cart track that led to the village Saunière remade nearby as a modern highway. He purchased houses and land. He and Marie kept open house for the local gentry, and persons such as Emma Calvé were known to visit. Generally both he and Marie lived high, with Saunière careful enough to cover his tracks. Title deeds were put in Marie's name, and the inscriptions on the Blanchefort grave- and headstone he obliterated (not knowing that a written copy had previously been made).

The mayor called round again, superficially angered at Saunière's treatment of the tomb, but in truth curious as to his new-found wealth. Saunière fobbed him off, with food, wine and cash, as was also the case with the bishop of Carcassonne, who himself came snooping. Undeterred, Saunière went on with his projects. He built a villa, with ramparts and a tower, where he installed an extensive library. Soon after that the then bishop of Carcassonne retired. His successor, a Monsignor de Beauséjour, was a little more forceful, and demanded to know the source of Saunière's wealth. Saunière prevaricated. The bishop had him summoned to the court of Rome, and suspended. A new priest came to Rennes-le-Château, but was given the cold shoulder – not only by Saunière, but by the villagers, whose loyalties hadn't changed. Eventually the bishop accepted defeat.

In January 1917 Saunière arranged for a new water supply to the entire village, work that he himself didn't live to see carried out. He died on 22nd January of cirrhosis of the liver (all that high living), leaving Marie as his sole beneficiary. That left Marie as the only person who knew his secret – which meant Marie was richly provided for throughout the remainder of her life. She shut herself away, and for many years lived as a recluse. In 1946, a M. Corbu and his wife came to live with her. To M. Corbu she related her fantastic story. She promised him her house and told him his future was certain to be secure, while not exactly saying how. The bad news for Corbu was that this never happened. In 1953 Marie suffered a stroke, went into a coma, and died. The result was that neither Corbu nor anyone else has known how to recover the treasure – until, that is, now.

4 The clues

Of the parchments that Saunière found, two of them were apparently genealogies, dating from 1244 and from 1644. Two others were the work of one of Saunière's predecessors – Abbé Antoine Bigou, curé of Rennes-le-Château – who had composed them in the 1780s. One other role for Bigou had been as personal chaplain to the Blanchefort family, who until 1789, when the Third Estate declared itself, and the Bastille was stormed, owned land locally and were powerful nobles. Bigou is said also to have designed the Blanchefort tomb referred to in the previous chapter.

Of the two Bigou parchments that Saunière found, the first has a concealed message that is not that difficult to uncover. Its text is organised in such a way that some of its letters occupy a horizontal plane slightly higher than those alongside them. When read in sequence, this is the message these letters form:

A Dagobert II Roi et a Sion est ce tresor et il est la mort

or with accents –

À Dagobert II Roi et à Sion est ce trésor et il est là mort

or

This treasure belongs to Dagobert II king and to Sion and he is there dead

An alternative reading of là (meaning 'there') is la (the definite article), which would render a significantly different emphasis on the entire sentence, which shouldn't be overlooked:

This treasure belongs to Dagobert II king and to Sion and it is death

(Dagobert as we have seen was the Merovingian Frankish king who came to his throne in 676, and whose lineage by 711 was in hiding in the Razès.)

The French word 'à' can mean 'at' as well as 'to', which would give us 'king at Sion' rather than 'king to Sion'. The word 'il', or 'he', in 'il est là mort', could mean 'He' (as in the Lord, i.e. the king at Sion), which in my mind establishes the connection between Rennes-le-Château and Jerusalem not as the Priory of Sion but as Jehovah, or something attributed to the cult of Jehovah, awaiting rediscovery somewhere close to Saunière's church. If we interpret 'il est la mort' (rather than 'là mort') as 'it is death' then this could mean that whatever is concealed is of a dangerous or destructive nature, perhaps some hazardous piece of knowledge, device or natural element, in a place closely connected with, or in fact resembling Jerusalem (a point I will explain in due course).

The second parchment consists of a cipher whose meaning is not as simple to discover – is in fact murderously difficult. Saunière's paleographers established that it required a key – a key that Saunière found, then carefully removed from the Blanchefort tomb. The inscription found on the tomb's headstone showed many obvious errors in its lettering, and it was these apparently erroneous elements that when gathered together formed the phrase 'mort épée'.

The cipher itself is a text from the Gospels into which 140 extra letters have been inserted. The middle 12 of these you have to discard, with the remaining 128 set out according to a standard cipher system, which is known as the Vigenère. To these the key phrase 'mort épée' is applied. This now produces another set of letters, in themselves meaningless, and which are all then shifted one place forward in the alphabet (so for D read E, for G H and so on). That results in another new configuration, requiring another key. That key is the complete text of the headstone, plus two letters from the gravestone. Reverting to the Vigenère, but applying the key backwards, and ending with the two extra letters, results in another series. This too is shifted, this time by a factor of two alphabetical places.

The next step requires that the new set of letters is divided into two groups of sixty-four each. The first sixty-four are laid out on a chessboard. What one then does is select the correct starting square, before executing the only sequence of chessboard knight moves that will cover the whole board by landing on each square once only. The second group of sixty-four is treated in the same way, but the repetition is undertaken in reverse, mirror-wise. From this the final message emerges. Not only that, the message is confirmed as an anagram of the text of the headstone that provided the key. All too highly complex perhaps, but this is the message:

> Bergère pas de tentation que Poussin Teniers gardent la clef pax DCLXXXI par la croix et ce cheval de Dieu j'achève ce daemon de gardien à midi pommes bleues

or

> Shepherdess no temptation to which Poussin Teniers hold the key peace 681 by the cross of this horse of God I complete this demon guardian at midday blue apples

Much in this message has defied explanation, though it does offer one good reason why Saunière acquired his copy of Poussin's *Shepherds of Arcadia*. The painting depicts a shepherdess and three shepherds next to a tomb in a pastoral setting. The tomb is inscribed with the phrase *Et in Arcadia Ego* (I, too, am in Arcadia) – a phrase also quoted on the Blanchefort gravestone, though in a form linguistically disguised.

Arcadia as a real location is a mountainous region in the Peloponnese, in Greece. In Greek mythology it came to be regarded as home to the pastoral god Pan, and was eulogised in classical times – and in the Renaissance – as an earthly paradise. Its pastoral character coupled with its geographic isolation in part explains why that was so. *Et in Arcadia Ego* is a phrase that refers to death, present even in this idyllic place.

There was, until 1988, not far from the churchyard at Rennes-le-Château, a tomb very like the one in Poussin's painting. That seemed to call into question the standard view among Poussin historians, who have largely assumed that the tomb and its landscape were of Poussin's imagination. However, but for certain details, the landscape depicted in the painting closely corresponds to an actual view – as a kind of Arcadia-Rennes-le-Château conflation. Nearby is the hill with the ruins of Blanchefort, which the painting shows. From the spot where the tomb once was, you can see, on the right horizon, the small hill on top of which Rennes-le-Château is situated, which Poussin also includes. There is one detail he doesn't match, and this is a rising slope in the mountains to the left. In the painting this is a slope that falls.

There is other interesting material connected with Poussin. In 1656, the Abbé Louis Fouquet addressed a letter to his brother, who was superintendent of finances at Louis XIV's court. The letter describes a meeting with Poussin, suggesting that through him it was possible to gain advantages that even kings would covet, and which, in the centuries to follow, would be extremely difficult to rediscover. (In that light, it's little surprise that one of my co-researchers interpreted the painting, and the shepherds within it, as guardians protecting a coffer.)

Taking all the evidence – and not the least of this is the cipher from parchment two – it is an almost inescapable conclusion that one of Poussin's underlying purposes was as a pointer to the mystery of Rennes-le-Château. One can only wonder at the full extent of his connection to it.

The author Henry Lincoln, from research underpinning books that he's written on the subject – notably his jointly authored *The Holy Blood and the Holy Grail*, and his solo effort *The Holy Place* – details his own pursuit of Poussin in a trail to Shugborough Hall, which is in Staffordshire. Here he says was an earlier version of Poussin's *Shepherds of Arcadia* (not a copy). With that he suggests there might also have been a painting by Teniers. Teniers produced many works whose subject was the temptation of St Anthony. However, the painting Lincoln describes as having once been at Shugborough Hall doesn't involve the temptation theme – rather it depicts Sts Anthony and Paul, furthermore with a background shepherdess. From this it is no daring leap of the imagination to make a connection with the decoded parchment two (Shepherdess no temptation).

Lincoln discovered another link at Shugborough Hall. In the grounds is a stone structure on which is sculpted a version of Poussin's *Shepherds of Arcadia*. The reproduction isn't exact, principally because it's reversed – that's to say it appears as a mirror image. The stonework encompasses one other cipher (to add to those we've seen), which no one has so far decoded. Its figuration is the letters OUOSVAVV flanked on the left by a D and on the right by an M. The monument was put there in the eighteenth century – for what purpose no one seems to know.

There happens also to be a natural connection between Rennes-le-Château and Staffordshire. That part of England, as is the area round Rennes, is rich in halite or rock salt, which is present in soft layers of rock known as marls. In the latter nineteenth century brine pumping was a key industry to this English county, though with its tendency to accelerate the natural subsidence that occurs in areas of rock-salt this, as an activity, was largely discontinued by the late 1960s.

Bedded salt deposits are nearly horizontal, beds ranging in thickness from a few to several hundred metres, while salt domes, known as diapirs – having flowed under pressure and heat up through the overlying sediments – have evolved into vertically elongated deposits. These can be two to three kilometres or more in diameter. Geologically, rock salt mines are often ideal for storage of archived documents, and nowadays petroleum products and even radioactive waste. The method employed in mining is called 'room and pillar'. Salt is excavated by blasting, then out-loading rectangular entries and cross-cuts. Pillars from the original salt, in something like a chequer-board design, remain to support the roof of the mine. Rooms in bedded salt mines can be three to fifteen metres high, while rooms in domal mines can easily exceed thirty metres.

Interestingly, in central Europe, the geological periods associated with salt formation are ones that are also characterised by marine deposits, a detail Saunière may have been thinking of when he placed a fossilised sea creature in his museum. The geology of central Europe is of possible significance to Rennes-le-Château in other respects, not least because it is home to the Rhaetian Alps, situated mainly in the Graubünden canton in eastern Switzerland. It might be stretching the bounds of nomenclature to associate the name Rhaetian with the name Rhedae (by which Rennes-le-Château was previously known), until we discover that to the west of Graubünden is a place called Sion. Curiously, the Rhaeto-Romance dialects of south-east Switzerland and western Austria are also of the Rennes-le-Château area. Close to Sion there is a salt mine at Bex, where in the fifteenth century saline springs were discovered. The Swiss had no access to salt up till then and were dependent on others for their supplies. Bernese invaders into the region in 1475 started the exploitation using evaporation techniques, an activity that continued for nearly 200 years. Between 1684 and 1823 mountain excavations took place, and in 1836 larger deposits were found near Basel, though mining continued at Bex using bore-hole methods. Perhaps Sion had its own such shafts.

The Swiss Sion has one further feature of interest to us. There is a tower there looking very much like Saunière's Tour Magdala, forming part of a building called the Château de Tourbillon. There are two sites at Sion – a castle on one hill and a church on another, both at about 150 metres altitude, in the valley of the Rhône. One could imagine that the castle, now a ruin, sits on a plug of rock, beneath which is a salt mine. The castle tower is similar in its situation to the Tour Magdala, and the main window of the latter echoes in design terms three windows on the Swiss tower.

§

Shugborough Hall was begun in 1693, and was enlarged in 1748. In the grounds of the hall are a number of follies. One of these is a triumphal arch, not that dissimilar to the monumental gate of the Châteaux des Ducs de Joyeuse at Couiza. At Shugborough is a Doric temple, and at the château, flanked above its door, are two Doric columns, on either side of which is a frieze. There is also at Shugborough a pillar-like monument, not difficult to view as an aniconic representation of Jehovah and Abraham, or even a pillar of salt.

If the regions around Rennes-le-Château and Couiza share the same or similar minerals, could the Anson family, whose home Shugborough was since 1720, have been involved jointly in the same or parallel trade with the Joyeuse? My guess is that the unbroken cipher OUOSVAVV, with those flanking letters D and M, inscribed at Shugborough Hall, represents a chemical code, a code including oxygen and sodium. We shall return to this at a later stage.

It was only in the 1960s that Shugborough Hall became National

Trust property. Baron George Anson was born there in 1697, and was a British admiral. His four-year voyage round the world is noted for its feat of naval heroism, where a major problem he and his crews encountered was one characteristic of his era – i.e. the inability to establish longitude at sea.

The concept of longitude, as I shall demonstrate, is a not minor component of the solution to our treasure hunt.

5 Symphonie pastorale

Rennes-les-Bains, just a few kilometres from Rennes-le-Château, is a thermal spa, known to the Romans as such, and enjoyed today for its apartments and built-in complex. That comprises jacuzzi and steam room, a fitness centre and a swimming pool with temperatures topping eighty degrees. There is access too to thermal treatments, sometimes the necessary palliative for all those aching muscles, on those many days I have spent searching out clues to Saunière's treasure, up and over the rocky summits. Rustic walks along the ravine have been made that much easier through the introduction of stone platforms, put there after the floods of 1992 – a natural disaster that destroyed much of the church cemetery and gardens, and also one or two buildings. Nevertheless, no place affords better relief for weary Westerners – the peace and the quiet – all within striking distance of the region's many ancient sites, such as the ruined castles of Blanchefort and Coustaussa, or that of Arques, a perimeter wall bounding a rectangular enclosure with square keep, which in 1999 was being restored.

The name Paradise Pass – this is on the N613 to Narbonne – conjures exactly its character. The road passes the turn to Termes, which was a massive Cathar stronghold, whose round towers along the perimeter walls date from the twelfth century. The towers and walls enclose what remains of the keep, now a ruin. In the thirteenth century the whole château was embroiled in a four-month Cathar resistance to the Albigensian crusade. Past Termes the road careers on through Corbières wine country, to the Mediterranean, important waterway so crucial in the thirteenth century, for its trade routes to the East, north Africa and Spain.

Lesser roads winding from village to village pass through forested hills and spectacularly coloured spurs of rock. You see birds of prey hang and hover on the thermals, sometimes perfectly still, as if the whole landscape were fixed permanently to a single split-second – a temporal degree zero. The country is steeped, as we have seen, in ancient history – whose atmosphere seems to persist, inducing with it a sense of awe. Here I always feel powerfully the loss of our simpler evolutionary values – of a life once centred on local concerns and our sovereignty as individuals.

That expression once given to local life, in the formation of hilltop villages like Rennes-le-Château, is best appreciated from the road approaching Couiza. One can't help but think that it must have been a labour, living there, with that wearisome necessity of making the trek down, at regular intervals, to gather provisions. Perhaps those so domiciled in ancient times never imagined ever leaving the spot (has it not been said that the top of a mountain is the closest point that heaven is to earth?).

One has to think again – of the advantages our hilltop inhabitants enjoyed over their counterparts in the valley. Those below must always fear for their safety. Outward communications could always attract intruders, with an eye to plunder. A close look at Rennes-le-Château reveals no ancient houses built into the hillside. A more permanent life was lived at the mountaintop – therefore one asks, what order of human being would seek the sanctuary of that high place?

To reach Rennes-le-Château involves a climb either on foot or by horse, or ascent by car from Couiza up a very steep incline. Once the ascent is made, the reward is a breathtaking view. That makes it easy to forget that life here in past centuries was mostly hard and meagrely rewarded – until, that was, chance and coincidence brought their transformations.

Rennes-le-Château is about eighty kilometres south of Carcassonne – as we have seen in mountainous country. Generally mountain elevation is from 400 to 1,000 metres, variation occurring within relatively short distances. Due to the fact that the Spanish border used to lie eighty kilometres north of its present position, the area is littered with the ruins of magnificent old castles, such as those at Termes, Durban, Aguilar, Peyrepertuse, Puivert and of course Montségur (which is only to name the most familiar). It is often assumed that the castles were built to protect Carcassonne. However, could they have been protecting something else, a secret, a route to a particular place? And bear in mind too that by their sheer immensity, these places were designed to thwart intrusion, repel any threat, and to facilitate swift passage from the East as well as from the West.

The castle at Rennes-le-Château does pose certain historical problems, since it isn't obvious why it should have been built here at all, or what it is of value its fortifications protect. Add to this that in all high places the lack of fresh water is inimical to permanent occupation – unless sources can be tapped and culverts built – and the question only deepens. It would have to be pointed out also that the positioning of each of the other castles I have mentioned, unlike this one, does afford access to water. It therefore appears that in all other cases, settlement was thought of in the long term.

My 1986 Michelin guide doesn't give to Rennes-le-Château any particular quality that might distinguish it from the places around. For that, one has to view it from Couiza, at a height and a distance, standing back. From Couiza, the Rennes-le-Château skyline is very unusual, due to the height of its buildings and their orientation to the north. One can see too that Rennes-le-Château is built on land looking like a flattened dome – a not very common contour.

I have reflected many times, nudging my car into the rough, makeshift car park under the Tour Magdala (a tower built by Saunière), on the place's utter uniqueness. In the light of the late afternoon, the stonework powders itself in a dusting of gold. The sun in the west, a fiery globe as it sinks and gradually sets, can only be more or less as our ancestors had seen it, uncluttered by our modern cityscapes – our dwellings, flyovers and workplaces. Likewise the planet Venus, a morning or evening star.

A great deal has gone on – for example the church roof is newly restored – and Rennes-le-Château now attracts a good many visitors, all I suppose eager to share in the mystery. Certainly questions remain unanswered. Why, for example, did Saunière decorate his church interior so garishly, and certainly not in keeping with Catholic tradition? French churches in the Lot area, with the exception of Cahors cathedral, are stark by comparison, and don't measure up, say, to the richness so typical of English country churches. Over the last twenty years or so the industry that has grown up round Rennes-le-Château hasn't missed out on details like these. There have been way-out or weird ideas added to a burgeoning literature, all it seems on an exponential growth since the appearance of *The Holy Blood and the Holy Grail* (which in itself offers a controversial theory as to Saunière's secret). Much that is written on the subject I can't help think has caused either amusement or consternation among the local populace, and perhaps a few anxious moments for the scholars and historians, whom I envisage attempting to piece together and understand more about Bérenger Saunière, who could never consider leaving his last posting at the top of the mountain.

Of course in my own way too I add to the many outpourings, which exist as books, magazine and newspaper articles, all with their own particular slant or insight. Yet what I can offer, without recourse to clichés – secret societies, flying saucers or Mayan fugitives – is an orderly sifting through the evidence, and the solution it points to.

6 Brief survey of the Christian controversy

Baigent, Leigh and Lincoln, in *The Holy Blood and the Holy Grail*, show not only a penchant for secret societies, but having lit the fuse, and retired to the safety of the page, stand at one remove from the powder keg they have so effortlessly wedged into the foundations of Christianity. Prime among their hypotheses – or this may be derived from other sources (such as Christian apocryphal literature of the third and fourth centuries) – is an elaborate argument for a Christ who escaped his crucifixion, and for a spouse in Mary Magdalene who with the children he fathered left the Holy Land and travelled to France.

According to this idea, and the ethos of his times, Jesus would have sired several offspring, who on fleeing the Holy Land after the 'crucifixion' supposedly found shelter with their mother in a Jewish community, somewhere in the south of France. Here they perpetuated their bloodline. This therefore prolonged Jesus's lineage, which in the fifth century is supposed to have got itself intertwined with the royal line of the Franks, which as we have seen at one point made its mark historically as the Merovingian dynasty, of which Dagobert II was a later king. When Dagobert died, or rather was assassinated, it was supposedly the church that colluded in this – a spot of skulduggery that, but for the implications raised by Messrs Baigent, Leigh and Lincoln, would represent only the tiniest blot on a more widely blood-stained copybook.

However, this didn't quite wipe the Merovingians' holy slate clean, since the bloodline persisted partly through the Carolingians, and partly through Dagobert's son, Sigisbert, whose descendants included Guillem de Gellone (ruler of Septimania), and eventually Godfroi de Bouillon (who captured Jerusalem in 1099, the outset of the Crusader period). Godfroi's mythologised ancestry plays a part in the tales of Lohengrin, who according to legend was summoned from the temple of the Grail and borne on a swan-boat.

Our three authors muse as to how correct this hypothesis might be, and seem to suggest that it is. That being so, we can now regard the Holy Grail as existing as two things simultaneously. It is Christ's bloodline *and* his Europeanised descendants, of which or whom we can now view the Templars, whose cynosure is the Priory of Sion, as appointed guardians. It is also the vessel that received Christ's blood – meaning, not that metallic object apropos of which all Arthurian enterprise must now be futile, but Magdalene's womb (which in purely spiritual terms seems all a bit visceral). From this it is self-evident, to some people, that all those Gothic cathedrals, as monumental manifestations of the womb of 'Notre Dame', were shrines to Christ's consort, rather than to his mom.

Should that seem to undermine the mystery of Rennes-le-Château (for really it's something tangible we're after) our trio go on to say that the Holy Grail may have been something else in addition. When, in 70 CE, after the Jewish revolt, the Romans under Titus sacked the Temple of Jerusalem, much of its treasure was pillaged. This is celebrated in a carving on Titus's triumphal arch in Rome, which shows his army processing through the streets, and bearing aloft some fine examples of its plunder – a seven-branched candelabrum, a gold table, some musical instruments. The Baigent-Leigh-Lincoln axis thinks there may have been documents too – birth certificates, marriage licences and so forth, detailing these and other of Christ's rites of passage. It means we must now regard the Messiah as an aristocrat – which in a thousand-year ancestry, uncertainly traced to the House of David, perhaps wouldn't automatically be the case. However, it is an important point, since you'd find nothing like this in the Temple relating to, well, just any John Citizen.

Now should this all seem to bear strange and forbidden fruit, why not go the whole way, and speculate that if the Temple housed these articles, then why not his body too, or his tomb? Needless to say, our three authors do make this proposal, so that now the Holy Grail is four or five things. (Just can't keep up.)

That the Temple documents weren't destroyed is explained by the fact of Titus's soldiers, big-footed empire men, with an eye only to booty, who weren't all that interested anyway. Therefore as a vital remnant perhaps this documentation remained hidden – or with Baigent, Leigh and Lincoln let us say did remain hidden.

That brings us in consequence to the notion of a Holy pedigree, dormant in Europe, but intermittently re-emergent through organisations such as the Freemasons, which prompts this whole hypothesis to extrapolate itself in the defiles of a unified Europe, run, we are told, as a theocracy. In this set-up all processes of governance, unbeknown to a mere electorate, reside with the Priory of Sion – latterday mayors of the palace (I'm tempted to say) – pulling all the strings of our very own European Union, which to date the commissioners of Brussels have managed to disguise as a mere bureaucracy – or is it the case that in politics you do get these unholy holy alliances?

The Fanthorpes in their book (Patricia and Lionel Fanthorpe: *The Holy Grail Revealed*) object to all this on theological grounds, since it necessitates the crucifixion as a fraud in one of two ways – either a fake-up, cleverly stage-managed, or a deception wholly dependent on a hapless Simon of Cyrene, who was called on to impersonate the Messiah *in extremis*. The Gospels make it clear that as a part of his sentence Jesus was beaten and scourged. According to Ian Wilson, in his book *Jesus: The Evidence*, this means he was lashed with a pellet-studded whip. Too weak as a result of this to carry his cross-beam to the place of crucifixion, a bystander, Simon of Cyrene, came to his aid. For Baigent-Leigh-Lincoln this translates to 'was crucified in his place'.

For the Fanthorpes, either scenario doesn't exactly give us the best character reference for one of the world's great spiritual figureheads, whose entire ministry can mean very little now should we accept a postmodernist revision. Ian Wilson argues rationally against an illusory resurrection, and quotes David Strauss, a nineteenth-century Tübingen lecturer, who in his *New Life of Jesus*, published in 1865, pointed out that a phony Messiah, half dead and weak and ill, and in serious need of medical attention, would hardly reappear in and around Jerusalem as anything but that.

If we do accept recent revisions, that must give rise to all kinds of fantastic speculation. For one, if the Merovingians *were* descended of Christ, then it's no more improbable that that particular dynasty found itself in possession of a Christian relic or two, notably the Holy Grail (whatever that concept or object might be). Thereafter it's an obvious corollary to plump for Rennes-le-Château as somehow a repository for such a relic, however many hands it may have passed through via the Merovingians. And again, we can go further in this whole incredible rig-up, and claim for the Merovingians a direct connection with the House of David. David was born in Bethlehem, in Judah, and died circa 962 BCE, in Jerusalem. He was, after Saul, the second of the Israelite kings, and reigned circa 1000 to 962. He established a united kingdom over the whole of Israel, with Jerusalem as its capital. He became, in Jewish tradition, the ideal king, who founded an enduring dynasty, a figure who raised messianic expectations, with Jesus – symbolising the fulfilment of those expectations – later shown by the New Testament writers (point hardly lost on Baigent, Leigh and Lincoln) as being of David's lineage. But what is so important about David?

David began his career at the court of Saul as an aide. He became a close friend of Jonathan, Saul's son and heir, and the husband of Michal, who was Saul's daughter. He distinguished himself as a warrior against the Philistines, to a point that aroused jealousy in Saul. A plot was hatched to kill him. He fled to southern Judah and Philistia, where with wisdom and prescience he began to make plans for his future career.

He lived the life of an outlaw on the desert frontier of Judah, and became the leader of other such outcasts. So organised, the group endeared itself to the local population, by protecting them from other outlaws, or recovering their possessions when taken. If sometimes reliant on Philistine kings, for protection against Saul, David did maintain status as a patriot in the eyes of Judah's people. By various political gestures he also found favour with many Judaean elders. He waited, and was eventually 'invited' to become king – first by Judah in Hebron, later by all Israel. Moreover, in this, he wasn't regarded as a rebel against Saul, but as Saul's successor – a situation arising naturally when Saul and Jonathan were slain in battle against the Philistines.

On entering Hebron, and proclaimed king, David found himself rival to Ishbaal, Saul's surviving son, who had been crowned king. Civil war ended with Ishbaal's murder, at the hands of his own courtiers, leaving David heir to all Israel, which included the tribes beyond Judah. He conquered the walled city of Jerusalem, then held by the Jebusites, and made it the capital of his new united kingdom. He defeated the Philistines, who were never again a serious threat. He annexed the coastal region. He established an empire, with himself overlord to the many small kingdoms bordering Israel. His reign lasted almost forty years.

One of his main achievements was to unite the Israelite tribes, with himself as ruler over all. This was a break from tradition, which had seen the Israelites cohere in loose tribal confederacies. Each tribe was a collection of clans, and a clan was an expanded family. Thus the Davidic empire was in stark contrast to that. How did David do this? First by success against the Philistines, then by establishing the city of Jerusalem as the centre of power and worship. Jerusalem – or the 'city of David' – became for all Jews the Holy City. The royal line or the 'house' of David symbolised the bond between God and the nation, with the king as mediator between the deity and his people. In later times, Israel awaited a messiah – a new mediator. Christianity, in regarding Jesus as the son of David, gave notice that the messianic hope had been fulfilled, with David still at the centre of wider religious faith.

Israel's God was Yahweh, and David made that name supreme, to displace all others. Yahweh had created the world. He ruled the nations. He had established kingship as a means of that rule, with Zion the seat of his king. Moreover Yahweh was himself enthroned on Zion, with his king at his right hand – a nicety not unconnected with the Ark of the Covenant, which according to tradition Israel had borne through the wilderness. David brought it to Jerusalem, a rectangular wooden box, which supposedly embodied the presence of Yahweh. The Ark, Yahweh and Yahweh's regent David therefore confirmed Jerusalem as the Holy City, with David himself a kind of messianic prototype.

What could all this add up to, if we tempt ourselves with the Baigent-Leigh-Lincoln proposition? What that particular trio would seem to imply is that the Roman sack of Jerusalem in 70 CE, followed in 410 by Alaric's march on Rome (Alaric the Visigoth), has resulted not in the dispersal of Jerusalem's decorative treasures alone. Sensationally, what we might also consider is the prospect of a latterday Merovingian, whose seed is traced to the House of David, waiting to reclaim his throne, with the further implication that Yahweh himself – or some sort of representation of him – is somewhere dormant, tucked up for a long millennial night together with his covenants – perhaps even in Rennes-le-Château.

7 Earthly powers

Of course, one problem with the whole edifice of Christianity is in knowing when to take its pronouncements literally, and when to regard them as symbolic. Something many may feel it important to decide on is an authentic genealogy of Christ, who as fruit of a virgin birth can't technically belong to the House of David. Dismissing the virgin birth is to discount also the Messiah's divine parentage, which apart from resuscitating the spectre of various Christian heresies, would tend to reduce his mission to something vaguely moral or political. That then of course makes a book like *The Holy Blood and the Holy Grail* just another chapter in the annals of human conflict, at whose centre is a struggle for power, leadership and the rights of succession – all those things still dragging on in a post-Marx era.

If Christ himself was divine – and this has been a central question to those heresies we've touched on above – then Christ's brother James most would argue was, by contrast, mortal, and as son of Joseph could have been of David's lineage. Here again we can look to Ian Wilson, who points out inconsistencies in the Gospel according to Matthew, in tracing ancestry from Abraham, to David, to Jesus's flesh-and-blood family (*Jesus: The Evidence*, Chapter 4). That aside, Roman Catholics do regard James as the Apostle James the Less (though others see these as separate figures), who together with Peter became leader of the Christian church in Jerusalem. James was reputedly put to death by the Sanhedrin, the Sanhedrin being no less than the Jewish central religious and legislative council. (Words like 'reputedly' tend to be convenient, when performing as catalyst to brand new histories.) When the Epistle of St James stresses that faith without action is valueless, we have plenty of scope in dreaming action up. Is it, under the Baigent-Leigh-Lincoln guiding star, worth asking what became of James? Could we construct some similar thesis, and pack him off to

France?

To my mind, a more fruitful line of inquiry is that advanced in a later work, not by the same trio, but by two members of it – Michael Baigent and Richard Leigh – whose *The Dead Sea Scrolls Deception*, first published in 1991, sets out clearly what they and many others regard as the scandal surrounding the so-called Dead Sea Scrolls. First what are the Dead Sea Scrolls? These are a collection of Hebrew and Aramaic manuscripts, the first of which were discovered in a cave near the north west shore of the Dead Sea. This occurred in 1947, and those who made the discovery were shepherds (we recall Ignace Paris). The manuscripts were the property of the Jewish community at nearby Qumran, and had probably been hidden shortly before the Roman depredations of 68 CE. The scrolls incorporate fragments of almost every book of the Hebrew Bible, including the oldest known manuscript of the book of Isaiah, a commentary on the book of Habakkuk, a manual of teachings and rules of discipline for the community, and what is known as the Temple Scroll, which sets out in detail how the ideal temple of Jerusalem should be constructed. There are too other biblical, sectarian and apocryphal writings, which vary in importance and are not all in the same state of preservation.

Until their discovery, the oldest surviving biblical Hebrew manuscripts dated from the ninth century CE, which it goes without saying has made the Dead Sea Scrolls hugely important to Old Testament scholarship. Since 1949, excavations at a site called Khirbet Qumran, meaning 'Qumran Ruins', have uncovered the remains of buildings, which some scholars believe were once occupied by a community of Essenes. Who were the Essenes? They were a sect who detached themselves from the rest of the Jewish community in the second century BCE, as a result of Jonathan Maccabeus (and later Simon Maccabeus) usurping the office of high priest, encompassed in which was not only religious but secular authority. When the Essenes stood in opposition to this they were persecuted, and so were obliged to flee to the wilderness. This they accomplished with their own leader, the Teacher of Righteousness.

Some scholars maintain that the Essenes established a monastic community at Qumran at some point in the second century before Christ, perhaps during the reign of Simon (circa 143-134). Set apart, as were other Essenes in Judaea, the Qumran community resorted to apocalyptic visions involving the overthrow of Jerusalem's priests, followed by their own succession – not merely as the true priesthood, but as the true Israel. They immersed themselves in scripture, and they busied themselves with manual labour, worship and prayer. Their meals they took in common, as prophetic celebrations of the messianic banquet. Their baptism rite was a symbol of repentance and entry to the company of the 'Elect of God'.

In Herod the Great's reign (37-4 BCE), an earthquake and fire (in the year 31) prompted the temporary abandonment of Qumran, though the community did return. It remained until 68 CE, when under Vespasian the centre was destroyed by Roman legions. The site was garrisoned by Roman soldiers until about 73 CE, and rebels under Bar Kokhba were based there during the Second Jewish Revolt (132-135).

It was a French archaeologist, Roland de Vaux, who in the 1950s led the Qumran excavations, and it was these that revealed among other things an extensive aqueduct system, sourced by the Wadi Qumran, and filling up to eight internal reservoirs or cisterns, as well as two baths. The main building occupied the eastern part of the ruins, and this comprised a sizeable tower constructed of stone and brick. To the tower's east was a large room with five fireplaces. To its south, in one room, benches were discovered, and in another was evidence of a scriptorium (a bench, mud-brick tables, inkwells). A stretch of aqueduct and a reservoir separated the scriptorium from what may have been a refectory. Abutting this was a pantry, and in it were hundreds of pottery jars. Also identified were a potter's workshop, two kilns, an oven, a flour mill, and a stable. Living quarters were limited. A cemetery nearby held the remains of about a thousand adult males, with two lesser sites reserved for a hundred women and children.

In their own scrutiny of the Dead Sea Scrolls, Baigent and Leigh draw on the work of one Robert Eisenman, a man who had studied comparative literature at Cornell under Nabokov (he of *Pale Fire* fame, a novel at whose centre is the discipline of textual interpretation), and who in the mid-1960s had graduated with an MA in Hebrew and Near Eastern studies from New York University. Eisenman also picked up, in 1971, a PhD in Middle East languages and cultures – this time from Columbia University – one of his specialisms being Palestinian history and Islamic law.

It was Eisenman who pointed out that scholarship surrounding the Dead Sea Scrolls rested with a small number of specialists, whose interpretation of them he had reason to question. This was because the construction de Vaux's team placed on the texts seemed at some points scarcely consistent with the historical evidence they offered, producing instead an exegesis suspiciously at one with Christian orthodoxy. This is important because, contrary to Christian orthodoxy, Baigent and Leigh's researches point to certain theological differences between James and Paul (James the brother of Jesus), and propose that although this led to the inception of Christianity as a new religion, it wasn't in fact the one that Jesus would have sanctioned. This is one striking detail that de Vaux and his team are said to have suppressed.

It is hard to draw any firm conclusions from *The Dead Sea Scrolls Deception*, other than one perhaps: that the Catholic church's insistence that the New Testament Gospels represent historical truth (rather than a basis of faith alone) is foolhardy and fantastic. What so often emerges from the *Deception* is a mixture of deduction and inference, with the Essenes as a far from isolated sect, whose appreciation of Judaic law is both moral and zealous, putting them at odds with Jerusalem's official temple hierarchy. That struggle the Essenes engaged themselves in was far from pacifist (for example, those Qumran fires were used for forging arms). The sect numbered among its individuals both James and Jesus ('I came not to send peace, but a sword'), and spoke of a 'remnant' – Jews who unlike their counterparts among the various other sects had remained true to Judaic law, and presumably unlike others would be saved. As we have already seen, in Manichaeanism, in the Cathars and the Bogomils (and have touched on in Arianism, and with the Visigoths), a material and spiritual dualism is not uncommon in the metaphysics of religion. According to Josephus (Jewish historian, priest, and soldier, who was born circa 37 CE), the Essenes regarded the soul as immortal, yet temporarily enmeshed in mortal and corruptible flesh, which only at the point of death is set free – precisely the belief Innocent III and later the Inquisition sought to eliminate, as one counter to the tenets of Christianity. Yet what brand of Christianity was bequeathed to the world? Well, according to

Baigent and Leigh, it's a brand cooked up through the distortions of an evangelising Paul of the New Testament's Acts, and one Paul merely attributed to Jesus. That leaves us with the paradox of Paul as the first Christian heretic, with perhaps something akin to the Essenes, or to Catharism – the 'Elect of God' – as truer to Christ, or truer to the 'Teacher of Righteousness'.

It is through this notion of a 'remnant', those who at the world's end shall be called to Israel, that I think we will find a key as to the purpose underlying the treasures of Rennes-le-Château, bearing in mind that earthly powers tend not to get established without first acquiring wealth. I think too this is something Saunière understood, and is demonstrable by the kind of life he led and the things he did on that hilltop. Here he left us clear indications as to his own, non-sectarian appreciation of the true Israel's calling, quite apart from his clues to its one other remnant – an earthly crock of gold...

8 Voices in the wilderness

...Assuming it is gold.Myself I don't feel quite qualified to say precisely what the treasure is, or even whose hands bore it to Rennes-le-Château, though I do think it's time for us to return to the parchment clues, to find out more about this treasure. We have already glanced at what might possibly underlie the first of these clues, which tells us, cryptically,

> This treasure belongs to Dagobert II king and at Sion and he is there dead

Let's now take a look at the other parchment, and at what we might deduce from that:

> Shepherdess no temptation to which Poussin Teniers hold the key peace 681 by the cross of this horse of God I complete this daemon guardian at midday blue apples

You will recall from Chapter 4 the discussion on Teniers, who produced many paintings whose subject was the temptation of St Anthony, but also that one of his works, allegedly traced to Shugborough Hall, doesn't involve the temptation theme. Rather it depicts Sts Anthony and Paul, and in the background a shepherdess. St Anthony does have a connection with southern France, and is also considered the founder and father of organised Christian monasticism.

He was born circa 251 in Koma, near al-Minya, Heptanomis, in Egypt, and died in 356, possibly on 17th January, at the Dayr Mari Antonios hermitage, near the Red Sea. His feast day is 17th January. Anthony was a religious hermit and one of the earliest monks, whose rule was in essence a first attempt to codify monastic life. He was a disciple of Paul of Thebes, and practised an ascetic life from the age of twenty. After fifteen years he withdrew into absolute solitude to a mountain called Pispir, which was by the Nile. He lived here from about 286 to 305.

He began his famous combat with the devil in the course of this retreat, having to withstand a series of temptations well known in Christian theology. He emerged in about 305, to organise the life of a group of hermits who had not only established themselves close by, but who were consciously his imitators. In 313, after the Edict of Milan, Christian persecution ended, and Anthony moved to a mountain in the Eastern Desert, between the Red Sea and Nile. The Dayr Mari Antonios monastery is still there. This is where he remained, receiving visitors and sometimes crossing the desert to Pispir. He went twice to Alexandria – lastly circa 350 – to preach against Arianism.

Arianism was an heretical doctrine teaching that Christ the Son was not of the same substance as God the Father (a variation on the dualism theme). It was first proposed early in the fourth century by the Alexandrian presbyter Arius, and didn't disappear from the empire until 381, when the second ecumenical council met at Constantinople, and Arianism was proscribed. If that ended the heresy in the empire, it remained with some Germanic tribes to the close of the seventh century. In our own times, some Unitarians might be considered Arians, being unwilling either to reduce Christ to mere mortality or attribute to him a divine nature identical with God's. The Christology of Jehovah's Witnesses is also a form of Arianism, with Arius a forerunner of Charles Taze Russell, the founder of that movement.

For the monks who followed Anthony into the desert, theirs was the vanguard in God's army. Through fasting and other ascetic practices, they aspired to the spiritual purity and resistance to temptation that Anthony came to characterise. Meanwhile Anthony's cosmic tussle was one against the forces of evil and against the devil. The devil might appear as a monk with bread during fasts, as a wild beast, as a woman, or as soldiers who beat him and left him for dead. Anthony endured it all, with such great fortitude that his temptations have not only entered Christian theology, but Christian iconography too.

Anthony's saintly popularity reached its height in the Middle Ages.

The Order of Hospitallers of St Anthony was founded circa 1100 near Grenoble, in south east France. This as an institution became a pilgrimage centre for people suffering from the disease known as St Anthony's fire, or ergotism – a kind of poisoning. Robed in black, and ringing small bells while collecting alms, the Hospitallers were a common sight in many parts of western Europe.

St Paul of Thebes (the other figure in the 'no temptation' painting) is also called Paul the Hermit. He was born circa 230 near Thebes in Egypt and died circa 341 in the Theban desert. His feast day is 15th January. Paul was an ascetic who is traditionally regarded as the first Christian hermit.

According to St Jerome, his biographer, Paul fled to the Theban desert during the persecution of Christians between 249 and 251. This was under the Roman emperor Decius. From then on he lived a life of prayer and penitence in a cave. Jerome considered Paul, and not St Anthony, to be the first Christian hermit. Anthony is said to have visited him when Paul was at a very advanced age, and later to have buried him, wrapped in a cloak that Anthony had been given by Athanasius, bishop of Alexandria.

Jerome, whose numerous biblical, ascetical, monastic and theological works had a profound influence on the early Middle Ages, is known particularly for his Latin translation of the Bible – the Vulgate.

The Teniers painting depicts the two saints seated under the partial shade of a rockface behind them. One of these two figures holds a staff, and this is crossed by a second, which is leaning on a rock. Among the articles set out on the flat upper surface of this rock is a skull, an hourglass, and a model of the crucifixion. Forward of the staffs, and leaning against the rock, are three books of varying size – one of which is open. There is a fourth book open in the hands of the figure not holding a staff, though he is looking away from this and more toward the crucifixion. Below him to his right is a flask and a dish. More to the background, and in a fully sunlit, open space is a shepherd or shepherdess, with a few sheep scattered about. Nearby is whitish water tumbling into a river. In flight is a bird, possibly a dove, with a piece of bread in its beak. One of these seated figures is dressed in a black cape over an orange-looking garment, and the other's attire is similarly coloured. Symbolically (see J. C. Cooper's *An Illustrated Encyclopaedia of Traditional Symbols*) black is associated with the planet Saturn, having lead as its metal, while orange is associated with the planet Jupiter, whose metal is tin. Historically these metals have played a significant role in alchemy, particularly in the quest for the transmutation of matter.

I hesitate to interpret this painting, beyond the obvious fact of its two seated saints. One might guess however that the hourglass is intended to show the time of day, as is the very short shadow cast from one of the staffs. The skull in Christian symbolism connotes the vanity of all worldly things. It means also the contemplation of death, and this has made it an emblem of hermits. Also in Christian symbolism, the skull with a cross is representative of eternal life after Christ's death on Golgotha. Golgotha, of course, means 'place of the skull', more specifically Adam's skull, which is said to be buried there. It has also become the emblem of Sts Francis of Assisi, Jerome, Mary Magdalene and Paul.

Since it was not uncommon, historically, for delicate, or secret, or dangerous information to have been transmitted through written or artistic symbolism, then symbolism must play a major role in unravelling the various clues either in Saunière's parchments themselves or in some of the things they refer to. One popular reference, which the Lincoln trio has elaborated to the point almost of a doctoral thesis, is the initials PS, which crop up time and time again – written in the parchments, inscribed on the Blanchefort tomb, and carved also on a stone (known as the Dalle de Coume-Sourde) found a couple of miles from Rennes-le-Château. There seems to be the broad assumption that these initials stand for the Priory of Sion, an organisation which, as we've seen, is said to be behind the formation of the Knights Templar. Not only that, we are asked to believe that since that time it has borne its own secret seed forward through history, appointing its own grand masters and setting about its task – whatever that task may be – according to a written constitution. The Lincoln team advances evidence that as a body it continues to exist, albeit shrouded in secrecy, and concealed under so effective a barrage of spurious street addresses and non-existent telephone numbers that any sane person must suspect at least the possibility of a hoax.

One has only to recall Borges's *Tlön, Uqbar, Orbis Tertius* – which opens 'I owe the discovery of Uqbar to the conjunction of a mirror and an encyclopedia' – to appreciate how simple a matter it is to weave historical facts into a private mythology. Borges's story in no small way involves Berkeley, who was bishop of Cloyne in 1734, and who denied the existence of matter. This was in a reply to Locke (1632-1704), whose conception of the universe was Newtonian and mechanistic, a place where material bodies conformed to a clockwork *modus operandi* – that is to say, a universe exhibiting solidity, figure, extension, motion or rest, and number. Among other things, these bodies operate on human sense-organs, and on the immaterial substance of human minds – all of which amounts to a conjunction in those minds of ideas. Therefore what we perceive as the world around us is not really the world around us, but only our ideas of it. To Berkeley this was repugnant, not least because, although as a system it allowed that God may have created the world, it did not require God's eternal supervision. This it was that led him to deny the existence of matter, maintaining that material objects exist only through being perceived, or to put it another way, through the act of perceiving them. That things don't cease to exist in our absence is Berkeley's proof for the omnipresence of God, who at all times perceives all things everywhere. It was in this way that for Berkeley the world existed as a divine syntax, through which any well adjusted mortal may commune with his maker.

In Borges's revision of Berkeley, Uqbar is an undocumented region of Iraq or of Asia Minor, one of whose heresiarchs had declared the visible universe either an illusion or sophism, and that mirrors and procreation were abominable because they multiplied and disseminated that universe. As the story develops, it emerges that Uqbar is a region of Tlön, and that Tlön is an invented country, the work of a secret and benevolent society conceived in the early seventeenth century, and numbering Berkeley among its members. As the society's work began, it became clear that a single generation wasn't sufficient to articulate an entire country. Each master therefore agreed to elect a disciple who would carry on his work and also perpetuate this hereditary arrangement. However, there is no further trace of this society until, two centuries later, one of its disciples is an ascetic millionaire from Memphis (Tennessee) called Ezra Buckley, who scoffs at the modest scale of the sect's undertaking. He proposes instead the invention of a planet, and with certain provisos – that the project be kept secret, that an encyclopedia of the imaginary planet be written, and that the whole scheme will have no pact with the impostor Jesus Christ (and therefore none with Berkeley's God either). The date of Buckley's involvement is 1824. The timing of events in Borges's story is approximately a century after that, when Buckley's encyclopedia is beginning not to be a secret, and as a kind of mirror is beginning to disseminate its own universe. I mention all this simply because Lincoln and his co-authors don't seem to have considered that the Priory of Sion could be a fiction along these Borgesian lines, especially as among its past grand masters Newton is numbered, as are Leonardo da Vinci, Robert Fludd, Robert Boyle, Victor Hugo, Claude Debussy, and Jean Cocteau.

As far as I'm concerned, PS is as likely to denote the sun's polar distance, or Polaris, as an element in astronomy – and astronomy, as is so often the case in mysteries of this kind, plays its own vital role in my search for Rennes-le-Château's hidden treasure. This is not to conflict with the view that Christian theological heresies, such as Arianism, or that practised by the Cathars, have at certain times been forced to secrete themselves, and carry out their programmes under a veil of self-protection – not always of course successfully. I would add to this that by now it ought to be clear that I accept wholeheartedly the suitability of a place like Rennes-le-Château for the pursuit of a belief and a way of life at odds with whatever have been the dominant powers. Its remoteness could hardly be bettered as the repository of anti-papal ideology. Furthermore its mountain summit could well have been considered one of the highest points on earth, a central location – a kind of paradise – a cloudy meeting-place where heaven and earth are merged as one.

Withdrawal to sacred mountains has come to symbolise renunciation of worldly desire, their summits conceived as the centre of the world, where from that centre the fountain of all waters springs forth. In Rennes-le-Château – not himself having quite renounced the world – Saunière built two fountains. Most researchers seem to agree that whatever it was he found – forbidden treasures or whatever

– it involved valuable objects for which he was able to realise cash. However he viewed this, and whatever his inclinations philosophically, Saunière would certainly have understood the many alternative forces for Christianity that had survived throughout Europe, and the risks their adherents ran. Furthermore circumstances in the seventeenth and eighteenth centuries had made it problematic for the secrets bound to such heresies to be retained by a few elect. It is for this reason that I do not find it at all difficult to accept that certain sensitive information may have had to be written symbolically into the pictures by Teniers and Poussin, and later encoded in the Rennes-le-Château parchments. I think too there is good reason (which doesn't involve the Priory of Sion) why Sion, or Zion, and more widely why Jerusalem, is also attached to the secret treasures of Rennes-le-Château. On that subject, it will be necessary to go a long way back – and to take seriously the two dogmas on which the faith of the Old Testament rests.

Do we – as surely the Essenes did – take literally the idea of Yahweh as the one God, who has chosen Israel as his people? This is something Isaiah, whose book forms one of the Dead Sea Scrolls, does speak plainly of.

9 'Peace 681'

The Book of Isaiah is one of the major prophetic writings of the Old Testament. Isaiah is identified as the son of Amoz, and his book is about Judah and Jerusalem in the days of Uzziah, Jotham, Ahaz and Hezekiah, kings of Judah. In 6:1, Isaiah received his call 'in the year that King Uzziah died' (which was 742 BCE). His latest recorded activity is dated 701 BCE. However, only Chapters 1-39 may be ascribed to this period, Chapters 40-66 being later in origin and for that reason known as Deutero-Isaiah (Second Isaiah). A further distinction may also be made between Deutero-Isaiah (Chapters 40-55) and Trito-Isaiah (Chapters 56-66).

The development of Chapters 1-39 was a gradual process, with its final form dating perhaps from as late as the fifth century BCE. In spite of the book's long and complex history, Isaiah's message is clear. He was absorbed in the cult in Jerusalem, with its exalted view of Yahweh, and was certain that only an unwavering trust in Yahweh – rather than in politics or military pacts – could protect Judah and Jerusalem from enemy intrusion – the enemy at this time being the Assyrians. He urged recognition of the sovereignty of Yahweh, and denounced anything that opposed or obscured Yahweh's purpose. He articulated Yahweh's judgement on Judah and Jerusalem, which was due to their unfaithfulness, but he also announced a new future for those who trusted in Yahweh – in fact the coming of a mortal messiah, a king in David's line.

The reigns of David and Solomon had been the high watermark of Israel's prosperity. Cracks appeared after Solomon, which had the effect of making David's reign look like a golden age, at least in retrospect. Isaiah promised that this was a reign that would one day return. There would be judgements, and a terrible chastisement, which only few would survive, Yahweh performing his work on Mt Zion and at Jerusalem, and thereafter sending a Davidic king who would rule in righteousness:

> And I will restore thy judges as at the first,
> And thy counsellors as at the beginning:
> Afterward thou shalt be called,
> The city of righteousness,
> > The faithful city. (1: 26)

There would be notice of Yahweh's new regent:

> Therefore the Lord himself shall give you a sign;
> Behold, a virgin shall conceive, and bear a son,
> > And shall call his name Immanuel. (7: 14)

If in the Old Testament Isaiah articulates the messianic hope, in the New it shall be fulfilled:

> For unto us a child is born, unto us a son is given:
> And the government shall be upon his shoulder:
> And his name shall be called Wonderful, Counsellor,
> The mighty God, The everlasting Father,
> > The Prince of Peace.
>
> Of the increase of his government and peace there shall be no end,
> Upon the throne of David, and upon his kingdom, to order it,
> And to establish it with judgment and with justice
> From henceforth even for ever.
> > The zeal of the Lord of hosts will perform this. (9: 6-7)
>
> And there shall come forth a rod out of the stem of Jesse,
> And a Branch shall grow out of his roots:
> And the spirit of the Lord shall rest upon him,
> The spirit of wisdom and understanding,
> The spirit of counsel and might,
> The spirit of knowledge and of the fear of the Lord;
> And shall make him of quick understanding in the fear of the Lord:

> And he shall not judge after the sight of his eyes,
> Neither reprove after the hearing of his ears:
> But with righteousness shall he judge the poor,
> And reprove with equity for the meek of the earth:
> And he shall smite the earth with the rod of his mouth,
> And with the breath of his lips shall he slay the wicked. (11: 1-4)

And in Luke (4: 18-19) Jesus read to his fellow-Nazarenes Isaiah's promise:

> The Spirit of the Lord is upon me,
> Because he hath anointed me to preach the gospel to the poor;
> He hath sent me to heal the broken-hearted,
>   to preach deliverance to the captives,
> And recovering of sight to the blind,
> To set at liberty them that are bruised,
> To preach the acceptable year of the Lord.

Isaiah prophesies a paradise restored:

> The wolf also shall dwell with the lamb,
> And the leopard shall lie down with the kid;
> And the calf and the young lion and the fatling together;
>   And a little child shall lead them. (11: 6)

> They shall not hurt nor destroy in all my holy mountain:
> For the earth shall be full of the knowledge of the Lord,
>   As the waters cover the sea. (11: 9)

Jerusalem awaits the prince of peace, a Davidic king, who shall bring peace to the world. Therefore for Isaiah, Jerusalem, or the city of David, was the seat of a prospective earthly paradise, whose own fulfilment was the fulfilment of the messianic prophecies. But what of those prophecies concerning the messiah's temple? And how could that be connected to the mystery of Rennes-le-Château?

One of Isaiah's most important prophecies concerns Mt Zion, the mountain of God. Verses 1-3, Psalm 48, read as follows:

> Great is the Lord, and greatly to be praised

> In the city of our God, in the mountain of his holiness.
> Beautiful for situation, the joy of the whole earth,
> Is mount Zion, on the sides of the north,
> The city of the great King.
>> God is known in her palaces for a refuge.

Zechariah, 14: 8-9, reads:

> And it shall be in that day, that living waters
> Shall go out from Jerusalem; half of them toward the former sea,
> And half of them toward the hinder sea: in summer and in winter shall it be.
> And the Lord shall be king over all the earth:
>> In that day shall there be one Lord, and his name one.

Isaiah 2: 2 prophesies:

> And it shall come to pass in the last days,
> That the mountain of the Lord's house
> Shall be established in the top of the mountains,
> And shall be exalted above the hills;
>> And all nations shall flow unto it.

§

From the cipher in Saunière's second parchment is the figuration 'peace 681', which to my knowledge no one has so far been able to interpret. In the St James Bible, each chapter is numbered in two ways, conventionally and as part of a rolling total – which means that St James's Chapter 681 corresponds with Isaiah's Chapter 2, in fact the chapter in which the prophecy immediately above appears.

Could this perhaps mean that Jerusalem has been made into Rennes-le-Château? Is its secret monastic order that of Israel, that of God and Zion, that of Jerusalem, an order descended from Yahweh's chosen people? After all, Isaiah declares (2: 7):

> Their land also is full of silver and gold, neither is there any end of their treasures.

10 Venus and the winter solstice

It is by no means certain why Christmas or the birth of Christ came to be celebrated on 25th December. The most likely reason seems to be that early Christians settled for a date that coincided with the pagan Roman festival marking the winter solstice – the *natalis solis invicti*, or 'birthday of the unconquered sun'. This is the point in the year when the days start to get longer and the sun begins its higher ascent of the sky. The Romans held their Saturnalia at around this time, with celebrations originally on 17th December (they were later extended to seven days). During this festival, all work and business were suspended, with slaves and masters changing roles, and slaves in particular given temporary licence to express themselves much as they pleased – which presumably included words and actions directed against their masters. Society's moral restrictions were relaxed, and there was an exchange of gifts.

In his *Jesus: The Evidence* (Chapter 3) Ian Wilson, in discussing the nativity of Christ, puts the winter solstice – according to the Roman Julian calendar – at 25th December. Appropriating that date as also the date of the birth of Christ might therefore have been justified (he notes) through the idea of Christ as the 'light of the world'. However, if implicit in the Roman Saturnalia is the seed of Roman self-destruction – with the power to subvert that the festival temporarily handed its citizens and slaves – could we seek some similar phenomenon rooted in the Roman church? I do not mean by this any overt Christian heresy, which in character tends to be clerical rather than vulgar, but a process of self-critique at work within the Christian populace itself. One fairly obvious example is that of Rabelais.

Rabelais was a French writer and priest. He was born in Poitou circa 1494, and died in Paris in 1553. He was known to his contemporaries as a physician and humanist, but is remembered by us

Plate 1.
View towards Rennes-le-Château, from where Poussin must have stood to paint the *Shepherds of Arcadia*.

Plate 2.
Looking east on leaving Rennes-le-Château.

Plate 3.
A possible stone salt pan, found locally.

Plate 4.
The entrance stonework to the Château des Ducs de Joyeuse at Couiza at the confluence of the rivers Aude and Salz.

Plate 5.
Looking towards the castle at Rennes-le-Château, from Sauniere's private garden.

Plate 6.
The key 41° window, overlooking the secret room of Sauniere's church.

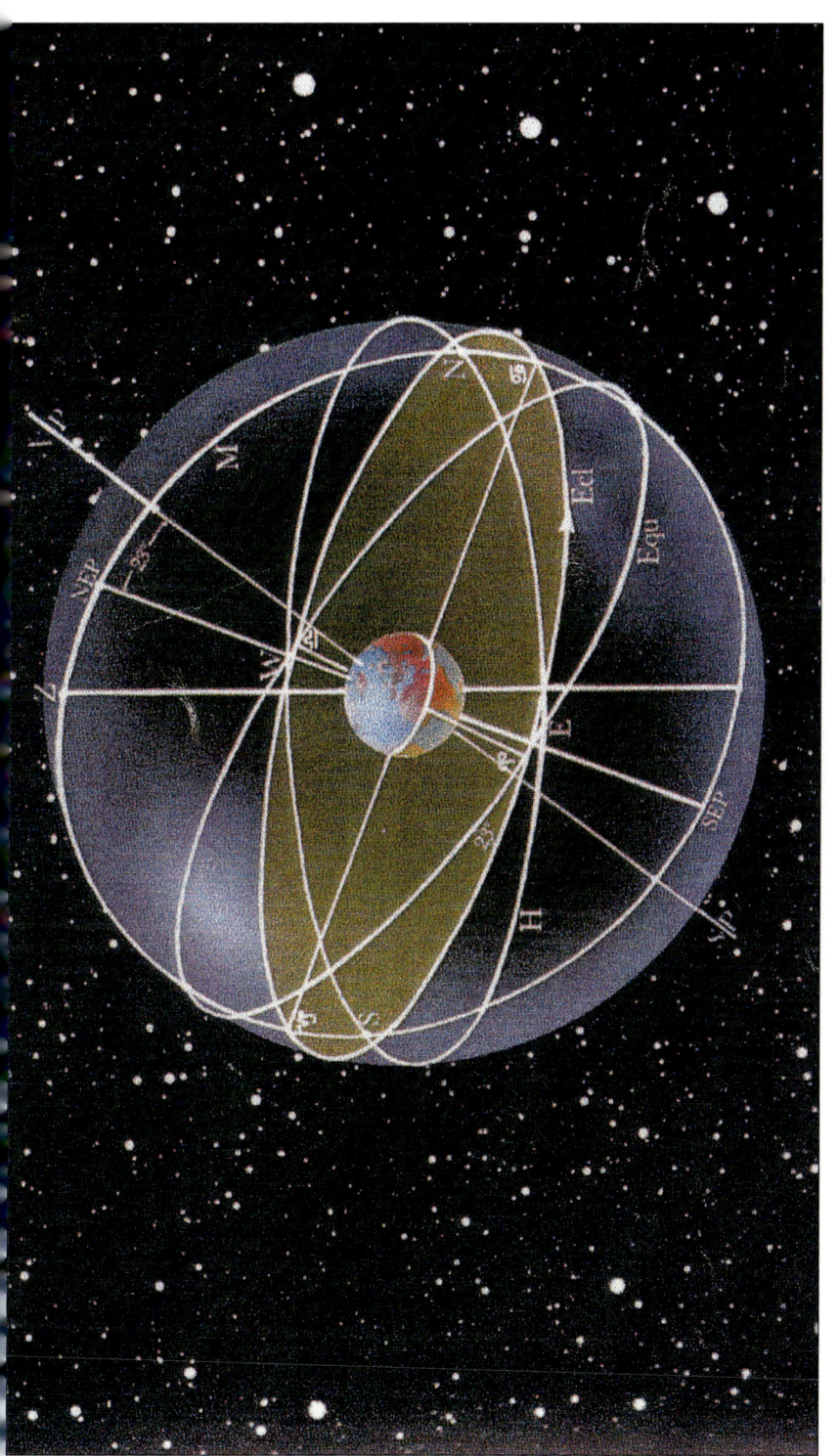

Plate 7. *(figure 1).*

The ecliptic is a secondary great circle that indicates the plane that the sun apparently follows on its journey around the earth.

Plate 8. *(figure 2)*.
Et in Arcadia Ego, Musée de Louvre, Paris.

as the author of *Gargantua and Pantagruel*, a comic masterpiece composed of four books, famed not solely for its rich Renaissance French, but also for its comedy. This ranges from burlesque to satire, and frequently in terms of profanities and oaths directed at sacred themes – for example the body of Christ, the blood of Christ, holy days, saints and relics, etc. In reading Rabelais it is sometimes easy to forget he was a monk.

§

There is no such dissent with our Teniers painting, one of whose seated figures is, as we have seen, St Anthony. St Anthony's feast day, as we saw in Chapter 7, is 17th January (17th January was also the day of Marie de Negri's death inscribed on the Blanchefort tomb). It is a date that also, according to the zodiac, falls within the last days of Capricorn, and Capricorn symbolically is the winter solstice. Its period is approximately 22nd December to 19th January, and is depicted not only by the goat. The crocodile, dolphin, animals with fish bodies, and the sea serpent are also its representatives.

Capricorn might also be associated with the virgin mother, or mother of God, who gives birth to the son of light – or Christ as the 'light of the world'. Light we can think of as bright in a golden age (such as David's), as departing at a fall or calamity (against which the prophet Isaiah pleads), and as returning when paradise has been restored. At the time of the winter solstice (which in the northern hemisphere is 22nd December, the first day of Capricorn), the moon is at its nadir, its lowest point, and Virgo rises in the east. Virgo – Latin virgin – is associated with the mother of Christ, and is variously represented as a fertility goddess or harvest maiden.

§

In astronomy the path that the sun apparently follows round the earth is known as the ecliptic. The plane of the ecliptic is tilted from the plane of earth's equator at an angle of twenty-three and a half degrees (it is this difference that produces our yearly seasons: see Figure 1). The farthest point south on the ecliptic is twenty-three and a half degrees below the equator, and is called the Tropic of Capricorn. The sun reaches the Tropic of Capricorn annually on about 22nd December, and it is this event that is called the winter solstice.

That twenty-three-and-a-half-degree angle is prime among the mathematical data supporting my theory as to the location of Saunière's treasure, having identified more than one instance of it in the various clues available to us. The first of these that I wish to consider is measurable in Poussin's *Shepherds of Arcadia* – as the angle at which the middle of the three staffs intersects the vertical (see Figure 2).

You can, if you wish, make this same angle central in your mapping of Rennes-le-Château and the places around it. Rennes-le-Château is positioned, more or less, at the confluence of several important routes. To its east you reach the Mediterranean, on a journey dotted with many of those castles I have already mentioned. From the Château de Ducs de Joyeuse at Couiza you can draw a line at twenty-three and a half degrees south east to Rennes-le-Château. The original position of the Couiza château was not fully exploited until 1231, when, during the Albigensian crusade, one Pierre de Voisins was placed in charge of the area. Likewise the castle at Rennes-le-Château became Voisins' property at that time.

In 1518, the last survivor of the Voisins family married a Joyeuse, and thereafter the site was able to realise its value. Construction of the château began between 1540-50. A short distance to the south, from the point one imagines that Poussin's painting was executed, close to the old French meridian – and the approximate location of the tomb – you can draw a line at twenty-three and a half degrees north east to the château de Termes, which dates to the twelfth century, and is now in ruins – round towers at intervals punctuating rectangular perimeter walls. When I was there, in 2000, it was still an awesome sight. I noticed the remains of stone cisterns, and wondered what was the alternative to these before they'd been built, especially in high summer or the frozen wastes of winter.

Its walls encircle the keep, which is the ruin's highest point. In the thirteenth century it was a Cathar stronghold, and one that resisted the Albigensian crusade for four months. After it fell it was made into a royal fortress.

From this same point on the meridian you can draw another line at twenty-three and a half degrees south east to the château de Peyrepertuse, a bearing that if extended would come very close to the château de Quéribus. The château de Peyrepertuse forms the largest ensemble of fortifications of its type in the Languedoc, and is a good example of the kind of medieval architecture found in this region. The château de Quéribus, dating to the thirteenth or fourteenth century, is a powerful polygonal keep with perimeter walls on a rocky summit. It was the last stronghold to succumb to the crusaders, and this occurred in 1255. It too was converted to a royal fortress, and stood guard over the Spanish marches until 1659, when the Roussillon region to the south became part of France.

A line drawn at twenty-three and a half degrees north east from Rennes-le-Château passes through Château de Durfort directly to Fontfroide abbey. Fontfroide abbey was founded by the Benedictines at the close of the eleventh century and became very prosperous. It was, in 1145, affiliated to the Cistercian order, and was a bastion of religious orthodoxy during the crusade against the heretics. Another line, which you can draw north east through Rennes-le-Château to Château Durban, will intersect the points Pech Cassou and Chateau de Blanchefort. This intersection is at an angle of about ten degrees. Following this line in its south westerly direction forms a further intersection with Montségur. When Montségur fell, over 200 of its Cathar faithful were burned at the stake.

There have been theories and speculation as to the meaning of other notional lines, in the geometric patterns they are said to compose. As far as my own inquiries go, what appears of most importance is the twenty-three-and-a-half-degree angle within the painting itself. This leads me to consider that Poussin, or perhaps the person who commissioned his painting, is trying to draw our attention not only to Rennes-le-Château, but generally to the workings (or to certain aspects at least) of our solar system. This has led me to think of the four figures in the painting as symbolic of one planet or another, which I am aware is quite a departure from Henry Lincoln's method of interpretation. Lincoln had the painting X-rayed, in an attempt to understand why Poussin had painted the left hillside as a descending slope, rather than as it is – that is to say rising. This led him to speculate that the underlying geometry that governs the painting is pentagonal, and is centred, approximately, on the shepherdess's forehead. Pentagonal geometry is important to the thesis set out in his book *The Holy Place*, which offers a convincing argument for a very large region, which encompasses Rennes-le-Château, in itself conforming to a geometry of pentagons – in the positioning of places and landmarks.

To my mind *The Holy Place* is certainly a recommended read. However, it shouldn't subsume Poussin solely into the realms of civic engineering and mystic temples, where Lincoln tempts us to incarcerate once and for all his *Shepherds of Arcadia*. One other level of analysis might just as well rest with the traditions of symbolism, which after all form part of the stock in trade of painters in practically any era. A book I have more than once referred to on this and other subjects is J. C. Cooper's *Illustrated Encyclopaedia of Traditional Symbols*, and via this I do not find it at all fanciful to identify Poussin's figures with some of the bodies in our solar system. His shepherdess I think represents Venus, able to appear in various forms, and usually dressed voluminously. Since Venus is a morning or an evening star, she is associated with both the solar and the lunar, and so is able to reconcile opposites. She follows the moon and precedes the sun. Her colours are green, pale yellow or turquoise. Her position is west, which is borne out here since the ridge to the right of the painting – already identified as Rennes-le-Château – is as viewed in a southerly direction. In astronomy, Venus is the second major planet from the sun, and is, after the moon, the most brilliant natural object in the nighttime sky. Venus comes closer to earth than any other planet in our solar system.

The shepherd in blue or violet I believe is symbolic of Mercury. Mercury is represented by the colour purple or deep blue, and takes as position the centre (as a mediator able to reconcile contradictions). The shepherd in reddish gold is the sun, whose age is young manhood, and the one in red is Mars, who is fiery, and whose position is south.

I haven't assumed that the painting and its symbolic representations can alone lead us to the point on the ground where the treasure is buried, though I do think it is intended for use in conjunction with some of the other evidence. Later I shall show its direct links to the geometry bound up in the second parchment, but for the moment shall demonstrate only what I believe to be the painting's clearest connection to the deciphered text of parchment two

> Shepherdess no temptation to which Poussin Teniers hold the key peace 681 by the cross of this horse of God I complete this daemon guardian at midday blue apples

– that connection being both 'shepherdess', which uniquely identifies one of the figures in Poussin's painting, and the term 'daemon guardian', which I interpret as spirit or genius of guardianship. Apart from all other symbolic meanings, Venus is the drawer of the bow and thrower of javelins, and constitutes a defence for the moon against the monsters of darkness – is in other words a daemon guardian. Her position in the painting – and we have to decide whether that is west, or in the Shugborough reversal east, or merely to the right in a purely pictorial sense – I intend to show corresponds with a very particular landmark on the ground in Rennes-le-Château, whose co-ordinate and orientation we have to uncover through our interpretation of the other clues.

11 Hermeneutics

Why can I not accept that Henry Lincoln's dissection of Poussin's painting can lead us to our co-ordinate? I will try to explain, but would like to preface that explanation with due acknowledgement of the ingenuity that has gone into his various analyses concerning Rennes-le-Château – his unravelling of the parchment ciphers, and how these are related to the stone inscriptions of the Blanchefort tomb and the Dalle de Coume-Sourde. He comes in *The Holy Place* to regard Rennes-le-Château as nothing less than the eighth wonder of the ancient world, at the heart of which is a geometric design conceived on an enormous scale. He traces a natural pentacle in the mountain peaks around Rennes-le-Château, and sees in this arrangement a man-made temple. This is a truly gigantic structure, sprawling for large distances across the landscape, in a configuration of pentacles, circles and hexagons, which in engineering terms Lincoln reasons must have involved far greater complexities than those overcome in constructing the Pyramids. He argues that having remained largely obscured for several centuries, the temple's presence and reality have been preserved for an exclusive elect. I can't disagree that there is in this monument – for what else would you call it? – something like a hieratic view of the world, not at all easy to uncover, and by design or chance submerged in a mass of cryptic clues. But why should a seventeenth-century painting obscure some of those clues in a way that requires X-ray technology – which of course didn't exist in Poussin's time – to uncover them?

Lincoln does at one stage associate Venus with Mary Magdalene (to whom the church in Rennes-le-Château is dedicated). He points out that she (Magdalene) was viewed by occultists in the Middle Ages as a medium of secret revelation, who regarded Venus as her cosmic symbol. He states that by chance there is a link between Venus, the pentagonal geometry he associates with the Poussin painting, and the area round Rennes-le-Château. This – as do my own expositions – involves observation of the planets, whose rotations round the sun are apt to form specific patterns. According to Lincoln, Mercury's solar conjunctions form an irregular triangle, while Venus's, over an eight-year cycle, form a pentacle. (Coincidentally eight in numerology is the number of paradise regained.)

Open as I am to the scope of Lincoln's findings, I still can't quite see why so much human ingenuity should have gone into the invention of an elaborate code and cipher system for the concealment of a monument only. Furthermore, since all these projections are a proliferation of X-ray analysis of Poussin's *Shepherds of Arcadia*, one has to ask how did a French Renaissance painter, who spent most of his working life in Rome, become interested in an ancient monument located in the south of France (supposing he did), and what was the extent of his knowledge of that monument?

The painting as far as I am concerned offers, in addition to a representation of Venus, one other important symbolic representation, and this is given us through the inscription on the tomb – Et in Arcadia Ego. Although straightforward as a translation exercise, the phrase can be made – through wordplay and trickery – to bear an unexpected meaning. 'Et' translates to 'and', 'both' or 'yes', and can mean 'than', 'also', or 'too'. 'In' means 'in', 'on', 'at', 'among'. 'Ego' means 'I'. Here is the interesting part. 'Arca' in Latin translates to 'box', 'money box', 'purse', 'coffin' or 'prison cell'. 'Di' means 'Deus' or 'God'. 'A' is 'from', 'after', 'since', 'by' or 'in respect of'. By this reasoning an alternative meaning of the Latin Et in Arcadia Ego would treat of the word Arcadia in its constituent parts – Arca-di-a. Hence:

> In respect of God's money box I too among

or

> I too have been with God's money box

Again according to Cooper, a tomb represents the womb of the earth, and is therefore associated with motherhood. Symbolism associated with motherhood is practically endless – water, fountains, wells – but from a Christian point of view is the virgin mother herself. It is worth pointing out also that in Christian symbolism both the tomb and the resurrection are represented by the altar – which allows us to think that Poussin's tomb might cryptically point to a church interior.

Mother mythology has associations also with the constellation known as the great bear, the plough, the big dipper or ursa major. This is a group of seven stars through which it is easy to locate the pole star, or Polaris. (Part of the inscription said to have been on the Dalle de Coume-Sourde is the phrase 'PS PRAECUM', which rather than having anything to do with the Priory of Sion could mean Polaris before all else.)

All this has led me to speculate on the importance of the tomb itself, as symbolising a repository – repository not of mortal remains, but of God's treasures on earth, or of treasures we have rendered to God. Such a repository could be a church (one has only to think of the sumptuousness of Roman Catholic ceremony), and that church could be Rennes-le-Château's. This at first was only speculative theorising, but it did turn out to be important.

Let's now take another look at the deciphered clue from the first parchment:

À Dagobert II Roi et à Sion est ce trésor et il est la/là mort

which has been popularly translated as

This treasure belongs to Dagobert II king and to Sion and he is there dead

In their book, *The Tomb of God* (1996), Richard Andrews and Paul Schellenberger point out that with linguistic changes wrought over time, alternative meanings to words can simply be lost – for example a glance at a nineteenth-century dictionary can render one interpretation of 'mort' as 'dormant'. This could therefore give us:

To King Dagobert and to/at Sion is this treasure and he/it is there dormant

– with possibly 'treasure' and 'he' or 'it' being synonymous with

Yahweh, or with the will of Yahweh, supposing we wish – and with a bit of imagination – to see this whole thing in the context of the Holy City. We do know after all that Dagobert's remains are somewhere other than Sion.

In summary then, I was beginning to explore the possibility of the location of the treasure as referenced by two or more co-ordinates – one of these associated with Saunière's church, the other with some kind of landmark associated with Venus.

§

It would have been impractical of course to seek out a fully elaborated co-ordinate system, whose function was to pinpoint Saunière's treasure, based on Poussin's twenty-three and a half degrees, without first understanding how far the science of astronomy had advanced during the seventeenth century. Was it possible, as I believed Poussin had done, to derive his angle either from the plane of the ecliptic to earth's equator, or from the sun's angle to earth at the time of the winter solstice?

Astronomy as a science was given its early impetus through the needs of marine navigation. Our present-day global co-ordinate system is defined by lines of longitude and latitude, and was borne of precisely these navigational needs. Lines of longitude are measured in degrees and minutes relative to the meridian through Greenwich, whose own measure is zero. In the early days of navigation, there was no reliable measure of longitude at sea, although latitude presented less of a problem. This could be measured as the angle between a celestial body and the horizon.

The north pole can be considered not only as a point on the Arctic, but as a position in the heavens directly above that. This – the celestial north pole, as it is known – is the point about which the stars appear to rotate (in reality it is the earth that rotates), and is very close to Polaris, the pole star. Latitude is the angle between the equator and the vertical, which is also the angle between the celestial north pole and the horizon. Thus, latitude can be established simply by measuring the angle between Polaris and the horizon. When Polaris is not visible, or if greater accuracy is required, any other astronomical object that is on or near the north-south line can be used, such as the sun near midday, or the moon, planets and stars. Navigational history is littered with a host of devices for making this measure.

The mariner's astrolabe is an early example. It was invented by the Portuguese in the late fifteenth century, as a derivation of the much older astronomical astrolabe (a two-dimensional model of the heavens with sights for observation). It consisted of a metal disc graduated in degrees, with a rotating sight vane pivoted at the centre. It enabled navigators to measure the altitude of a celestial body by aligning the sight vane to it.

A much cheaper instrument was the cross-staff, which came into general use during the sixteenth century. This was a long wooden shaft with a movable cross-piece. The navigator looked along the shaft, then moved the cross-piece till one end appeared to touch the horizon, and the other the celestial body, whose altitude was read from a scale on the shaft. The cross-staff was an instrument also employed by surveyors, to calculate heights and distances.

The English quadrant or back-staff – first described in 1595 – measured the altitude of the sun according to the shadow the quadrant cast. This was more accurate than previous instruments, and by the seventeenth century generally superseded the astrolabe and cross-staff. The mural quadrant evolved from this, and was very much larger – its size in fact was what gave it its improved accuracy. It was fixed vertically to a wall, the wall set north to south. The projection of the rotating arm swept out part of the observer's meridian on the celestial sphere. The arm was aligned to the celestial object as it crossed the meridian, with the altitude read from the arm's position.

Not quite the same ingenuity was so readily forthcoming on the problem of longitude – which is crucial in identifying the precise position of objects – ships, reefs, countries – on the globe. The issue wasn't satisfactorily resolved until the invention of John Harrison's marine chronometer. (Interestingly there is a link between the quest for longitude and Shugborough Hall, and, rather more loosely, the Blanchefort tomb, both of which I shall come to.) First though John Harrison. He was born in March 1693, in Foulby in Yorkshire, and died on 24th March 1776 in London. He was the son of a carpenter and mechanic, and he decided in 1728 to turn his hand to the construction of an accurate chronometer. Several disasters at sea, caused by poor navigation, had resulted in the Longitude Act of 1714, wherein Parliament pledged a £20,000 prize for anyone who could solve the problem.

The essence of the marine chronometer is this. In order to calculate longitude at sea, it is necessary for the navigator to know the time not only aboard ship, but at some other point of reference also (for example Greenwich). The difference between these two clock times allows the navigator to arrive at a geographical separation. If the earth takes twenty-four hours to complete a revolution, and that revolution is through 360 degrees, then each difference by one hour is equivalent to 15 degrees longitude. In John Harrison's era, this would require the navigator resetting his ship's clock each day to local noon – i.e. when the sun reached its highest point. That time he would then compare with the time given by the home-port clock. Until Harrison's intervention, no clock had been manufactured that was accurate enough to keep home-port time over a voyage of any distance.

Harrison's first chronometer was completed in 1735. He built three others, each smaller and more accurate than its predecessor. In 1762, on completion of a voyage to Jamaica, the last of these was found to be in error by only five seconds. Therefore, within workable parameters, the problem of longitude had been solved (a long time after Poussin's painting, but prior to the date inscribed on the Blanchefort tomb).

Shugborough Hall in Staffordshire, as we saw in Chapter 4, has in its grounds a bas-relief mirror-image version of Poussin's *Shepherds of Arcadia*. The stonework encompasses a cipher, the figuration OUOSVAVV flanked on the left by a D and on the right by an M. No one seems to know why, but the monument was erected in the eighteenth century. What links Shugborough Hall and the issue of longitude is that from 1720 it was the home of the Anson family. Baron George Anson was born there on 23rd April 1697 (he died 6th June 1762 at Moor Park, Hertfordshire). He entered the Royal Navy in 1712, becoming a captain eleven years after that. In September 1740, as a commodore, he set off across the Atlantic in pursuit of Spanish treasure ships in the Pacific, without a chronometer, and therefore largely on the strength of latitude readings. He had six ships – all poorly manned and ill-equipped – which he began to lose. By the time he crossed the Pacific, he and his surviving crew were down to one remaining ship, the *Centurion*. All suffered acute hardship while crossing the Pacific, though near the Philippines did manage to capture a Spanish treasure galleon. On his return to England in June 1744, more than half the original crew of nearly 2,000 men had died, chiefly of scurvy. These dietary problems were exacerbated by the navigational difficulty in measuring longitude, making stops for renewed provisions haphazard. (One other possible link between Shugborough Hall and the mystery of Rennes-le-Château is that apart from the Poussin bas-relief, a reproduction of Teniers' *St Anthony and St Paul* is said to have been lodged there.)

Prior to the introduction of Harrison's chronometer, a reliable method of calculating longitude was sought by astronomical means. A promising candidate was known as the 'lunar distance method'. Way back in 1514, Johannes Werner, a German astronomer, reasoned that the motion of the moon could be used as a means of determining location. Per hour, the moon travels a distance approximately equal to its own width, and in the daytime moves to or from the sun. Werner's idea was this – that if astronomers mapped the positions of all those stars that were on the moon's path, then predictions could be made as to which star the moon would pass at what time, for the years ahead. In the same way the relative positions of the sun and moon in daylight hours could also be mapped (the moon being up in the daytime for half of every month). Tables could then be published indicating the moon's travels, and the time, over a given meridian, of its conjunction with each star. Having that information, a navigator would then compare his own times and conjunctions with those in his published tables, and according to the difference in hours calculate his longitude. The problem that remained was the positions of the stars, which weren't that well known.

What all this was to lead to was an astronomer's co-ordinate system based on what are termed 'declination' and 'right ascension'. Unlike declination, which is defined much as described above (as an angular measure in the calculation of latitude), right ascension is measured in units of time. It has its basis in what is known as the first point of Aries. The first point of Aries is where the ecliptic and equator cross, which is reached by the sun, travelling south to north, on about 21st

March each year (the vernal equinox). It is this, the first point of Aries, that forms the prime meridian of the co-ordinate system. A star is said to 'culminate' when it reaches its greatest altitude in the sky over your, or the observer's meridian. The first point of Aries therefore culminates once a day, and right ascension is the time difference between that culmination and the culmination of the star you are observing.

It was Galileo, born in Pisa in 1564, who as mathematician, astronomer and physicist was the first man to use a telescope to study the skies. The telescope was a new invention in 1609, and on hearing of it Galileo built his own. It had a threefold magnifying power, which he quickly improved to thirty-two. In late 1609 and early 1610 he announced a series of discoveries – notably, that the surface of the moon was irregular, and that the Milky Way was a collection of stars. He also discovered the satellites of Jupiter, which he named Sidera Medicea, and he observed Saturn, spots on the sun, and the phases of Venus. Some of his first astronomical observations were published in 1610 in *Sidereus Nuncius*. Within two years of their discovery, he had tabulated the revolutions of Jupiter's satellites, and also put forward the idea that their frequent eclipses might be used as a means of determining longitudes on land and at sea.

Later, with John Flamsteed, came the kind of data Werner's method demanded. Flamsteed, who was born after the era of Poussin's painting (in 1646) founded the Greenwich Observatory, and was England's first astronomer royal. Poor health obliged him to leave school in 1662, from which point he studied astronomy on his own. From 1670 to 1674 he continued his education at Cambridge. Flamsteed is well known for his exhaustive observation of the stars. This amounted to a catalogue, a version of which, edited by Halley, appeared in 1712, and which in 1725 listed 3,000 stars and defined their positions more accurately than ever before. Halley succeeded Flamsteed as astronomer royal in 1720, and among the work he carried out was a design towards determining longitude at sea.

We can see therefore that the sixteenth, seventeenth and eighteenth centuries saw pioneering work in the study of the heavens, giving rise, particularly through the need to establish latitude, to greater and greater precision in the instrumentation used to measure the altitude of the sun and other stars. This latter was a procedure very well developed by the time Poussin came to paint his *Shepherds of Arcadia*, which Christopher Wright in his *Poussin Paintings* (1984) puts at about the late 1630s. There is a clear distinction between this painting, known as the Louvre version, and one earlier by Poussin on the same theme and subject. This latter Wright dates from the early 1630s, and is known as the Chatsworth version. Its appeal is more directly emotional and doesn't seem to be modelled on a Rennes-le-Château landscape, unlike the Louvre version, which by contrast is pervaded by a mood of contemplation.

In any event, given those approximate dates, I felt encouraged to continue my investigations in terms of geometry and co-ordinates.

§

If I was now following in Saunière's footsteps, had he or a possible predecessor left me any clues to confirm these frail beginnings of my theory? There are some that I feel are worthy of mention:

Astrologically, the symbol for Aries is the horns of a ram, and among Saunière's revised décor for the interior of his church is the figure of a devil whose head is sprouting just such horns. Also, the altar pillar in which the parchments were found has a distinctive 'Y' carved on it. There is, on the water tower at Rennes-le-Château (this is south of the car park), an impressive sundial, which shows among its calibrations marks for the solstices. Then, as we have seen in Chapter 3, there is the Blanchefort tomb, which dates Marie de Nègri's death as 17th January 1781, with her age at death being sixty-seven. That would put the year of her nativity at 1714, the year in which the Board of Longitude was set up. We may add to that that the day of her death is not only St Anthony's feast day, but falls within the scope of the last days of Capricorn (or winter solstice) for the year 1780. It was during the 1780s – or might well have been 1780 itself – that Bigou, Saunière's predecessor, is said to have composed the encryptions for the parchments.

I couldn't quite believe that all this was mere coincidence, given the extent to which Bigou had made use of the Blanchefort tomb (or probably even fabricated it), and I therefore thought it worthwhile to learn what I could of the winter solstice for 1780. Figure 3 shows the sun's declination during that event, and reveals also that the angle between the sun and Venus was forty-one degrees. This also is an angle that recurs elsewhere among the various clues, as we shall see.

12 Blue apples

As we know, once Saunière had uncovered the treasures of Rennes-le-Château, his greatly expanded living brought with it wider restorations, which included repair to the presbytery, a new wall round the churchyard, a rock garden, a summer house and fountain, and the five-kilometre track to the village upgraded to a highway. His alterations to the church included, over the door, a carved Latin inscription, which translated reads: 'This place is terrible'. The church interior became a mélange of tasteless décor – for example Christ salving the afflicted is portrayed near a money bag. That grotesque statue of the devil I mentioned earlier, complete with ram's horns, is not that distant from other statues – of painted angels, with glassy vacant eyes.

There is one other obvious point concerning Saunière's restoration, and that is the layout of his garden – its paths and landmarks – and the relationship this bears to a map of Jerusalem. (See Figures 4 and 5.) Jerusalem has, as its religious and mystical centre, the Templum Domini, the House of God on earth, or heavenly tabernacle – the place of communion between God and Israel. It seems quite clear that Saunière, in remodelling Rennes-le-Château, imitated in so far as he could certain features of Jerusalem – not only in name, but generally in orientation.

This would mean that the Calvary south of the church coincides with the Templum Domini. As I have demonstrated, I had come to view the church as perhaps in some way forming one of the co-ordinates necessary in locating Saunière's treasure, and with this borne in mind a part of the clue derived from the second parchment began to make a little more sense. I am referring to this:

> by the cross of this horse of God I complete this demon guardian at midday blue apples

– the key phrases of which I shall take step by step.

In 'by the cross' I interpret 'cross' as the Calvary south of the church. The Calvary of course is a model of the crucifixion, though one interesting point about the one at Rennes-le-Château is that the cross is ornamented with what looks like the sun and its golden rays. 'This horse of God' is by my reckoning the sun itself, which I deduced after consultation with J. C. Cooper again. I looked at the entry for 'horse' in the *Illustrated Encyclopaedia*, and found that according to Christian symbolism a horse does in fact connote the sun, and represents courage or generosity. Coincidentally in traditional symbolism white, golden or fiery horses are associated with solar power, and can appear drawing the chariots of sun gods. Fiery chariots represent ascent to heaven by the spirit, by divinities, or by holy people.

'I complete' I read as 'I fix', as in fixing something in place. 'Daemon guardian' I have interpreted already as the spirit of guardianship, and more precisely as Venus, or as something we associate with Venus. Recasting the whole phrase therefore gives us something like:

By the Calvary of the sun I fix Venus at midday blue apples

In the nautical almanac of December 1780 – and it was in 1780 that I am now assuming Bigou composed his encryptions – the declination and passage over the meridian are indicated for Venus, Mars, Mercury, Saturn and Jupiter, together with the moon's longitude and latitude at noon. The surprise is, however, that all these computations have a direct bearing on those last two words of the second parchment message – the blue apples. Why?

I did in fact stumble into many blind alleys here, before finally grasping the solution. I chased up a host of definitions. Blue for royal horse guards, the blues (emotionally speaking), blue stone, sulphate of copper, the colour of the Virgin Mary. Nothing outstanding there. Then apples, apple being the fleshy fruit of a roseaceous tree-quince – the 'apple' of Dionysus – fruit of the tree of life – given by Iduma to the gods – symbol of divination and immortality.

I took another look round the gardens of Saunière's church, for any vague clue to apples, blue or otherwise. Perhaps the fountain and water feature he had built there in some way corresponded to the central fountain of paradise. The sealed fountain represents the Virgin Mary, and her colour is blue. Water is the liquid counterpart of light. Blue apples could be divine waters, or they could form part of the design in a work of blue stained glass. The apple, in biblical terms, is likely to be the quince or apricot, which is sacred to Venus. The apricot is a symbol of self-fertilisation or androgyny. It is also a symbol of the philosopher's stone in Hermetic tradition – the attainment of unity, a regaining of the centre – Hermetic works being by nature revelatory, with subject matter ranging from the occult to the philosophical. For example the Hermetic concept of astrology treats the cosmos as a unity, with all its constituent parts acting interdependently... .

As you can see, early thoughts here were vague and inconclusive. I did though come to consider blueness in terms of light, or a blue filter for light. This led me to revisit the research I had carried out into navigational instruments, with a review of any device whose operation involved the reflection of light. There was of course the sextant (with its forerunner the octant), with its one fixed and one movable mirror – so this I bore in mind. However, for the time being, that's about as far as I got with that particular line of research, so I now took a further look at Saunière's private garden, with a view to its geometric layout relative to its position to the church. I also wanted to know what trees and other plants were growing, the orientation of the walls, the features of those walls, especially the church walls (for their windows and glass, and above all stained glass). I began to form the idea that if one stood at the window (supposing there was one) at the south side of the church, in alignment with the altar, or perhaps the Calvary (or both) at midday, or on the day of the winter solstice, or both, the sun's rays would light on something on a wall inside. Well, in fact, there was such a window, whose angle and position were such that a ray of sunlight passing through would be refracted through another, south-westerly window, onto a point inside the church.

I subsequently learnt that there is a raised or marked outline of black and white squares on the floor inside the church, which corresponds to the direction of this refracted ray of sunlight. I then came across a copy of Gérard de Sède's *Signé: Rose Croix*, whose subtitle is *L'énigme de Rennes-le-Château*. This was published by Librairie Plon, in a 1977 edition. Its text of course was in French, and bore up, on pp149-151, a description of a picture of blue apples, situated inside the church on the north wall. The blueness was said to appear only at a particular time of day, due to the angle of the sun's rays. Here in translation is that part of the text:

> Don't leave the church of Rennes-le-Château before studying the most astonishing of all the pictures that adorn it. This picture, made without canvas, or brushes, or colours, which appears each day, and each day removes itself, has been painted by a beam of sunlight.
>
> To see it requires fine weather. You position yourself inside the church, before the north wall, at exactly midday. You can see an image form on the wall, at first deceptively – but a tree covered with fruit. In transit from left to right, the image shapes itself so that the fruit seems to ripen before your eyes. When fully developed, you see a fine apple tree, all of whose fruit is red – except for three apples, which are blue. Then, little by little, the image dissolves again and spreads to the extreme end of the wall. The effect (which you can photograph) lasts exactly one minute and eleven seconds.
>
> What produces the blue fruit's appearance is the passage of a sunbeam at exactly midday through the central motif of a stained glass window in the south wall. Most surprising is that the motif – a leafy circle decorated with the initials of Bérenger Saunière – does not replicate itself either near or far from the image that has formed it. One can only admire the skill of the glassmaker, for the number of optical calculations that had to be performed in achieving the desired effect.
>
> The motif is repeated on the wall with the Tree of Knowledge, but slightly modified. At its centre the initials BS are effectively replaced by the sun. This prompts you to consider that it's the passage of the sun that demands your attention, and not the simple chance that the three forbidden fruits are pomegranates.

I felt, at last, I was on the right track. What I had to do now was put it all together – which in due course we will do.

13 Was Jerusalem builded here

Till now there has been no obvious explanation as to the choices Saunière made for his work of restoration. For example, what made him select those particular black and white floor tiles, which we looked at in the last chapter, or the garish art work that adorns his church interior? And are there any special principles involved in the design and layout of his garden? I believe I have the answer to these questions, with much of what Saunière left behind having more than a superficial meaning. I believe too that that meaning is connected with a mystical conception of paradise – as in a sense is Poussin's classical Arcadia. Moreover that is a conception formally enshrined in both the structure and religious importance of Jerusalem, but one apparently subverted in the emphasis placed on the teachings of Christ through the evangelising process of St Paul.

Let me take you for a stroll outside the church at Rennes-le-Château. It's worth just casting an eye over the surrounding countryside, which on a hot, slightly breezy sunny day, is idyllic. Allow me to point you to a detailed local map, through which you'll discover many hilltops capped with castles and other fortifications, such as at Montségur, with all its Cathar associations. Sometimes the atmosphere is palpably charged with the aftershock of all that doctrinal conflict, which one inquisitor (Bernard of Gui, died 1331) articulated as a tract directed against the Albigensians:

> It would take too long to describe in detail the manner in which these same Manichaean heretics preach and teach their followers, but it must be briefly considered here.
>
> In the first place, they usually say of themselves that they are good Christians, who do not swear, or lie, or speak evil of others; that they do not kill any man or animal, nor anything having the breath of life, and that they

hold the faith of the Lord Jesus Christ and his gospel as Christ and his apostles taught. They assert that they occupy the place of the apostles, and that, on account of the above-mentioned things, they of the Roman Church, namely the prelates, clerks, and monks, and especially the inquisitors of heresy, persecute them and call them heretics, although they are good men and good Christians, and that they are persecuted just as Christ and his apostles were by the Pharisees.

Moreover they talk to the laity of the evil lives of the clerks and prelates of the Roman Church, pointing out and setting forth their pride, cupidity, avarice, and uncleanness of life, and such other evils as they know. They invoke, with their own interpretation and according to their abilities, the authority of the Gospels and the Epistles against the condition of the prelates, churchmen, and monks, whom they call Pharisees and false prophets, who say, but do not.

Then they attack and vituperate, in turn, all the sacraments of the Church, especially the sacrament of the eucharist, saying that it cannot contain the body of Christ, for had this been as great as the largest mountain Christians would have entirely consumed it before this. They assert that the host comes from straw, that it passes through the tails of horses, to wit, when the flour is cleaned by a sieve (of horse hair); that, moreover, it passes through the body and comes to a vile end, which, they say, could not happen if God were in it.

Of baptism, they assert that water is material and corruptible, and is therefore the creation of the evil power and cannot sanctify the soul, but that the churchmen sell this water out of avarice, just as they sell earth for the burial of the dead, and oil to the sick when they anoint them, and as they sell the confession of sins as made to the priests.

Hence they claim that confession made to the priests of the Roman Church is useless, and that, since the priests may be sinners, they cannot loose nor bind, and, being unclean themselves, cannot make others clean. They assert, moreover, that the cross of Christ should not be adored or venerated, because, as they urge, no one would venerate or adore the gallows upon which a father, relative, or friend had been hung. They urge, further, that they who adore the cross ought, for similar reasons, to worship all thorns and lances, because as Christ's body was on the cross during the passion, so was the crown of thorns on his head and the soldier's lance in his side. They proclaim many other scandalous things in regard to the sacraments.

Moreover they read from the Gospels and the Epistles in the vulgar tongue, applying and expounding them in their favor and against the condition of the Roman Church in a manner which it would take too long to describe in detail; but all that relates to this subject may be read more fully in the books they have written and infected, and may be learned from the confessions of such of their followers as have been converted.

From *Bernard of Gui, The Inquisitor's Guide*, trans James Harvey Robinson in *Readings in European History*, Vol. I (Boston: Ginn, 1904), pp381-383

If this is a pause in our treasure hunt, it is not without a sense of this whole area round Rennes-le-Château as one steeped in the problems of faith, with its various sects and fraternities, rooted in or at odds with the ideals and prophecies cast with the very mortar of Jerusalem, with the Old and the New Testaments, with that perennial quest for the fruits and tranquillity of paradise.

As I have said, Saunière's Rennes-le-Château – that hilltop he re-created in a very distinctive image – is, in layout, strongly reminiscent of the Holy City, an impression very easily realised in a comparison of maps. *Carta's Historical Atlas of Jerusalem* (Israel Map and Publishing Co Ltd, 1976), by Dan Bahat, reproduces several of these in its chronicle of Jerusalem's changing fortunes from 586 BCE to the reunification in 1967. Rennes-le-Château's *Guide de la Visite*, my own copy of which dates from 1983, has its map too. Here are some of the similarities, or correspondences, which to me seem far from coincidental (Rennes-le-Château's features italicised): the *Tour Magdala*, David's Tower; the *emplacement forteresse*, St Mary of Mount Zion; the *ruines de l'église Saint-Pierre*, the church of St Peter ad Vincula. (See Figures 4 and 5.)

Back in the 1980s, I had formed the theoretical conviction that in Saunière's mind Jerusalem, Rennes-le-Château, and some sort of concept of paradise had become inextricably linked. I was now expecting to discover that his private garden had been set out to reflect that notion, and anticipated that the trees and shrubs within it would turn out to be the symbolic plantings of paradise. At that time I knew about his summer house and rock garden, and the decorative fountains, but hadn't yet seen where these features were in relation to the church. Also I had no idea how he would have managed a water supply. It was these questions I now wanted to address.

So, here's my inventory, compiled on 4th July 1983, some time between 4.00 and 4.45 p.m. Saunière's private garden lay south west of the church, and these were the trees and plantings growing there: hazel, vines, cherry, pear, apple, fig, Spanish chestnut, elderberry, wistaria, persimmon. Some of these he must have travelled some distance to purchase. As to any symbolism bound up in these choices, the fruitful vine represents fertility and passion, and in Christianity Christ is the True Vine, with his disciples the branches:

> I am the vine, ye are the branches:
> He that abideth in me, and I in him,
> The same bringeth forth much fruit:
> For without me ye can do nothing.
>
> (John, 15: 5)

Cherry, again in Christianity, is a fruit of paradise, and is often depicted with the infant Christ, while the pear denotes Christ's love of mankind. The apple, of course, is the fruit of temptation, and has powerful associations with sin and the fall. The fig and fig leaf we know from the garden of Eden, the chestnut connotes victory over temptation, the elder is to do with witchcraft (rooted out as a Christian heresy) and is an emblem worn on Walpurgis night, and the wistaria is a climber well known in English gardens. The hazel, as the tree of life, grew in Avalon, island where the legendary King Arthur went to heal his wounds. Incidentally Geoffrey of Monmouth's *Vita Merlini* (circa 1150) describes Avalon as 'the island of apples', in a possible association with Celtic mythological traditions of an Elysium (abode of the blessed after death). The name Avalon is close to the Welsh word for apple, afal. Sir John Rhys, in his *Studies in the Arthurian Legend*, linked the name with that of Aballach, a Celtic divinity. Avalon has also been identified with Glastonbury, and this may have a connection with Celtic legends about an 'isle of glass' – also a final habitation for dead heroes.

Saunière's fig trees grow all along the north wall of his garden, and his cherries along the south and east sides – these the extremities of his personalised paradise. The hazels are dotted round the fountain, and the fountain itself is positioned close to and south of the sacristy. I paced out the whole area, to arrive at rough measurements, and in so doing was strongly impressed that nothing had been put here as a result of idle whim. A Christian or mythological idea of paradise, and Saunière's general plan, are intimately related, and that I see as his purpose in transforming what was once a barren, unwatered hilltop. Over a hundred years have now elapsed since his garden was made, and its trees today provide deep shade against the heat of the sun.

Both pools – the fountain and child pool – lie south west of the church, with the water inlet to the fountain lying due south. On my visit to Rennes-le-Château in April 1984, I took the plan in the *Guide de la Visite*, and the layout of Jerusalem as it was in the Crusader period – 1099-1187 – and held them side-by-side. Here, to my mind, are the overlaps (in each pairing, Rennes-le-Château's landmarks are cited first): its *Tour Magdala* maps to Jerusalem's David's Tower; its *emplacement forteresse* corresponds to St Mary of Mount Zion; the *ruines de l'église Saint-Pierre* are positioned similarly to the church of St Peter ad Vincula. In Saunière's garden, on the western side, surrounded by a high wall or terrace, is a northerly path that turns sharply onto the east-west axis, which resembles Temple Street in Crusader Jerusalem. There is also a path that branches from this, and curves from its northern edge, which I would liken to the Street of the Furriers in Jerusalem.

§

Overall our main areas of interest lie south and west of the church, which if we want to persist with the Jerusalem analogy takes in the Templar Quarters. The Templars, according to *The Holy Blood and the Holy Grail*, undertook secret excavations underneath the Temple, and whatever they found there brought back to Europe. Is it perhaps at its replication, here at Saunière's Rennes-le-Château, that the treasure will be found?

We shall see.

14 Relics and remnants

Saunière, with his clues, signs, symbols, and what is a not entirely Christian décor adorning his church interior, may have been attempting nothing more than communication with inquisitive people like me, who in the eras succeeding his own find themselves curious to learn his secrets. If you agreed with the Baigent-Leigh-Lincoln theory, you could almost view the whole escapade as just another chapter in a continuing quest for the Holy Grail – not that I would choose from the many options these three have given us as to precisely what that object or concept is.

It was without doubt for the knights of Arthurian romance an object, possibly a shallow or wide-mouthed vessel (though its exact etymology is uncertain), in a legend probably inspired by Celtic and classical mythology. Here horns of plenty and magic life-restoring cauldrons are common. The first extant text to give it Christian significance – as a mysterious, holy object – was Chrétien de Troyes's unfinished romance of the late twelfth century, *Perceval*, or *Le Conte du Graal*. This involved the rustic knight Perceval, whose chief characteristic was innocence, in a tale that interwove the religious and the fantastic. Robert de Borron, early in the thirteenth century, enhanced the legend's Christian significance with his poem *Joseph d'Arimathie*, or the *Roman de l'estoire dou Graal*. Wolfram von Eschenbach gave it mystical expression in his epic *Parzival*, in an account where the Grail is a precious stone that has somehow fallen from heaven. Prose renderings of de Borron's works linked the Grail story more closely with Arthurian legend. *Diu Krône*, a thirteenth century German romance, made the Grail hero Sir Gawain, while the *Queste del Saint Graal* made it Sir Galahad. This latter work has had the widest significance of all, its essence transmitted to English-speaking readers through Sir Thomas Malory's *Le Morte D'Arthur*, of the late fifteenth century.

De Borron's poem told the Grail's early history, in a link with the cup used by Christ at the Last Supper, then later by Joseph of Arimathea to catch the blood from the wounds of the crucified Messiah. The *Queste del Saint Graal*, with its new hero, the pure knight Sir Galahad, was a quest or a search for mystical union with God. Only Galahad could look at the Grail directly, and there behold its divine or ineffable mysteries. There has been comparison here with the mystical teachings of St Bernard of Clairvaux, active through the first half of the twelfth century, among whose writings is a treatise on the doctrines and dogmas concerning the Virgin Mary (whose immaculate conception he didn't accept), a eulogy to the Knights Templar, and a rebuke to Pope Innocent II, to the effect that the church was losing its moral authority (a situation largely down to the pope himself). *The Queste del Saint Graal* gained in emphasis by making Galahad the son of Lancelot, so contrasting the story of chivalry inspired by human love (Lancelot and Guinevere) with that inspired by divine love (Galahad).

In *The Holy Blood and the Holy Grail*, the Baigent-Leigh-Lincoln triumvirate seems at the very least to suggest that the excavation carried out by the Knights Templar under the Stables of Solomon had as its purpose the recovery of a treasure or relic linked to the Holy Grail, which having been brought back to Europe awaits rediscovery at Rennes-le-Château. It's an attractive theory (but then fantastic theories usually are). Yet what if it's wrong, and the real mystery of Rennes-le-Château is much more to do with our human condition, and an endless attempt to find a congenial and satisfying way to live, in a paradise on earth? Less implausible perhaps, here follows my alternative analysis, which I offer perhaps not solely as an example of the ease with which almost any interpretation can be arrived at.

The Old and the New Testaments are bound by two principal dogmas. One of these is the messianic hope expressed in the Old Testament, and supposedly fulfilled in the New Testament, in the body and flesh of Christ. Jerusalem is central to both Testaments. However, with the evolution of the church (the Catholic church, which is founded on the teachings of Christ), it can and has been argued that that fulfilment hasn't properly taken place. This is demonstrated in the mires of corruption that the church has often got itself into, and the purely political and worldly powers that successive popes have wielded. Isaiah, among other Old Testament prophets, has talked of the fulfilment in terms of a remnant, or an elect. Catharism, which directly connects Rennes-le-Château and Jerusalem, also presented itself in terms of an elect, yet espoused an unorthodox Christianity. This was by no means radical or new, since the examples of Manichaeanism and Arianism show us how persistent this undercurrent has been. Therefore what is implied is a New Testament fulfilment that does not rest with orthodox Christianity, but with a body like the Cathars, who preserved their elect through a small number of people. A small such number of people continued to exist, and recruited into itself via clues and codes that only astute individuals could ever unravel. The power of the elect was conceived on relics or riches from Jerusalem. Those relics or riches are now at Rennes-le-Château. Saunière discovered them. Saunière wearied of orthodox Christianity, and with the power the relics or riches had given him retired from the world, and rather than join the elect (whose time anyway may long have passed), and as a corruptible mortal, lived out his remaining life in a personalised paradise on earth.

Too fanciful, you say? Well, perhaps – but by the mid-1980s I still had my planetary and co-ordinate theory to work out fully. This was a busy time in my life, and the visit I made to Rennes-le-Château although rushed was thoughtfully planned. It was April. I had only a couple of days. Fortunately these coincided with a break in the cold weather, and with good light and blue skies I knew I should have a clear perspective in my roam round the mountains. My flight to Toulouse was an evening flight, and from here I picked up my hire car. There were delays, and this meant that I arrived in Rennes-le-Château at 9.15 a.m., on the crest of an invigorating drive up from Couiza, and in a surge of icy fresh air.

I parked up by the water tower, on an area of rough ground. After a walk through the cemetery I entered the church. Here I noticed that the window above St Antoine de Padoue's niche, was missing – which was precisely the point where I envisaged my calculations would have to be made, and the co-ordinates drawn. I examined that painted devil with the ram's horns (to try to ascertain if the eyes were looking in any particular direction), and I looked also at the black and white floor tiles, which were set at points north-south, east-west.

I strolled around the grotto, which is due south of the church, and here took some pictures. There was a weather vane above the Calvary, whose alignment didn't appear to coincide with that of the church – which was east-west. The vane was situated on a north-south axis.

I retired to think these things over, leaving Rennes-le-Château briefly and crossing the valley to the narrow road leading to Coustaussa, the site of a ruined castle. From here I could look across to Rennes-le-Château, and at around midday – that's to say one o'clock (since clocks in April are an hour in advance of clocks in December) – I could see the sparkle of reflected sunlight in the glass top of Saunière's orangerie.

On returning I suffered a major disappointment. The whole of Saunière's private garden had been given over to an encampment of tents, for a military exercise. I spoke briefly to a man dressed in French army kit, and was told I couldn't gain entry due to a survey or reconnoitre. I took the number of the brown truck parked nearby, and have it still – 2234 LX 76. Those last two digits represent *département* – in this case Seine-Maritime, which is north west of Paris – though beyond that this is not a registration I have ever attempted to trace.

It was in Rennes-les-Bains that I secured a map detailing ownership of all land in Rennes-le-Château. I was advised that the present owner of Saunière's one-time residence was involved in tax problems, which made it impossible to make contact. Off on another tack then, and at this point still nursing my theories, I decided this might be the moment to take another look at the Poussin tomb near Peyrolles, which at that time still existed. Here it was easy to visualise the orientation of the canvas and the compass alignments discussed in Chapter 10. Next I visited the Castle of Razès at Arques, and after that on a walk round Couiza I noticed that the Châteaux des Ducs de Joyeuse boasts a similar stone portico to that found at Shugborough Hall.

Back at Rennes-le-Château I took a look at the tower with its massive sundial, which of course faces south. Perhaps its significance has gone unnoticed until now because for most people it can mean no more than a quaint and antiquated timepiece. To someone who is interested in plotting angles of the sun at midday it looks rather different. I took notes and made sketches, but only later tried to understand its decorative inscriptions, which may have had a message to convey.

It was soon time for me to head north again, through the haze and the breezy sunshine, to an old house we owned at Varaire, where I had some business to attend. The drive took me through familiar country, whose long and eventful history was much in my mind: Castlenaudry, Revel, Puylaurens, Gaillag, St Antoine, Caylus, Cahors, and back to Toulouse. To date I had come to no firm conclusions, other than a powerful inclination that Saunière's treasure was there to be rediscovered, and the fact that I felt able to summarise the important pointers to Saunière's secrets, which I list as follows:

a) the clues offered two things – symbolic meanings and a means of establishing co-ordinates

b) an important angle in arriving at co-ordinates appeared to be Poussin's twenty-three and a half degrees, which seems to be connected with c)

c) the co-ordinates seemed also to have something to do with the winter solstice

d) the 'shepherdess' from parchment two I had identified as Venus in Poussin's painting

e) important co-ordinates appeared to be the Calvary, something on the ground that could be associated with Venus, and something about the church that the 'blue apples' clue drew our attention to

f) the rationale underlying the treasure was very probably to do with Christian asceticism, of which the Teniers painting might be said to be one of several clues (St Anthony the hermit, etc.)

If at the moment all this was very inconclusive, I did have a sense of satisfaction that at least I had taken a lingering look at the place where the abbé had lived out his final days – perhaps secure in the knowledge that his wealth was without end. I could not help but regard his as a personal destiny uniquely resolved in a paradise that he himself had constructed.

In 1984 I came across a book lodged with the archive study documents in Rennes-le-Château, called *Les Cahiers de Rennes-le-*

Château. It had been printed in Nice in 1984, and published by a firm called Collection Belisane. It was written in French. In part it was concerned with Saunière, and discussed some of the Latin inscriptions supposedly composed by him, and which had been engraved in and around his church. One of those inscriptions starts like this, and is carved in Latin over his church door: *Regnum Mundi Et Omnem Ornatum Soeculi Contempsi* – a phrase whose exact wording is also found in Thomas à Kempis, in his *Imitation of Christ*. The *Imitation* emphasises the virtues of the spiritual life, and is an exhortation to despise the material world.

> I have despised the kingdom of the world and all worldly attractions

So sings the novice on the day vows are made in a convent or monastery.

Thomas à Kempis was a monk, who took his vows in 1408, was ordained in 1413, and who devoted his life to copying manuscripts and to directing novices. Here I quote him again:

> For the sake of My Lord Jesus Christ, whom I have seen, whom I have loved, in whom I have believed, in whom I have delighted

It seems possible to me that rather than indicate by these engravings Saunière's devotion to Christ (either spiritually or as the Grail or a mummified relic), oblique reference is being made to his acceptance of a monastic order – not of course the kind of orthodox order to which Thomas à Kempis belonged – but a remnant, and one whose existence parallels conventional Christian thought. On this premise, one could therefore take the view that Saunière has tried to show himself as someone bound by an inner solitude, in part secular, the foundation of which he had already passed on to Marie Denarnaud when he died. The clues he left were clues as to why the treasure was there, and as to its precise location-point, which he had determined from the evidence of Poussin, and of the parchment ciphers.

15 Last visit to Rennes-le-Château

Having got this far, the pressures of work and the demands on my time meant several years before I was able to return to Rennes-le-Château – nor had I written on the subject quite as I'd wished. This state of things didn't exactly facilitate my calculations in the location of the chamber, vault or trove – which was proving difficult. I began to think there was something I had overlooked – but what?

From a news flash, some time during the early 1990s, I learned that Rennes-les-Bains had suffered badly in a storm. The village appeared to have been engulfed, and what was really a deluge had left a great deal of debris. Mindful of the links between Rennes-les-Bains and Rennes-le-Château, I began to fear for the latter too. I was anxious to return, but didn't get the opportunity to do so until 1999. By coincidence I had met an old friend and colleague of mine, Farooq Hasan, who because of me was himself seduced into the mystery of Rennes-le-Château.

Farooq had been a sea captain, and was naturally a widely travelled man, though nowadays worked independently as an entrepreneur. We decided to pool our resources, and felt that in working together the secrets of Rennes-le-Château wouldn't elude us for very much longer. We settled on a joint visit, and set the date for July 1999.

Farooq's perspective differed from mine in its almost exclusive focus on the spiritual. Mine was on navigation and astronomy – with a little land surveying too. When we sat down later together, we were able to discuss the whole mystery in quite some depth.

We met up, and took the Eurostar from Waterloo. In Paris we took the train to Cahors, which is north of Toulouse, and was the place where we broke our journey for the night. I had other business in the village of Varaire, where my family had previously owned a small property, and so next morning we set off relatively early in a hire car. We left Cahors behind, in itself an ancient place, with a history closely intertwined with that of the Knights Templar, and headed for the country roads off the N20. After Varaire, we entered the Aude *département*, passing through Cordes, Carcassonne and over the bridge at Couiza. Thirteen years had passed since my previous drive down here, but the turn-off for Rennes-le-Château was so much the same, and so indelible a memory, those years simply melted away, and were more like hours.

The red soil round Rennes-le-Château flanked our zigzags up the mountain roads. The craggy rock formations dotting the wooded hillsides took on a slightly rosy tint in the intense summer sunlight. We arrived at the village by late afternoon, after a 250-kilometre drive, from whose hilltop the views, as ever, were staggering: the wooded mountains, the bunched fists or solitary fingers of rock, a turquoise haze on the hilly contours inking the horizon, the farms, hamlets, the occasional stone ruin.

There had too been some changes. Cars could now be parked on the rough ground south west of the presbytery, and the garden east of the Tour Magdala had been opened up. This constituted a major alteration, since it had been impossible in years past to gain access here. I retraced an elevated route leading to the greenhouse, which I found had deteriorated badly, with scarcely a pane of glass remaining. We took our bearings, then the two of us headed off for Rennes-les-Bains, where we checked into our hotel. I had stayed previously in a hotel nearby, called the Thermal Roman, which had a new name now and had seen extensive renovations. We ate there late. There was, we thought, evidence of the water I had seen reported in the news flash, though fortunately not that much.

In part this was a holiday, and next morning we drove along the road to Arques. Our first stop was at the point beside the D613 where Poussin's Arcadian tomb – or one resembling it – once used to be. It was destroyed in 1988, because its then owner found no other remedy for the many grave robbers that recent publicity had attracted to it. Nevertheless, we were able to gauge the point at which you'd imagine *Shepherds of Arcadia* having been painted – not in fact close to the tomb's position, but on an elevation north of the road, where a ravine cuts its course beneath. Although from here you can relate the ridge of Rennes-le-Château to its representation in the painting, there is no such resemblance in the range that according to Poussin rises above the tomb's left extremity. This is visible between the two shepherds who are clutching their staffs. Also you can't make much sense of the hill to the left of the painting. I personally have seen the original twice – once at the Royal Academy, and once at the National Gallery. Perhaps this is fanciful, but I do sometimes think that Poussin painted his own profile and represented it in this painting as an undulating hillside. That would therefore give us another self-portrait – of a French Renaissance painter, forty years in Rome – a genius at odds with his times (man after my own heart!) – but laid to rest in a personally constructed paradise. And a painting within a painting.

We continued on our journey to Arques. There we visited the castle, which had once been the property of Simon de Montfort's lieutenant – a rectangular enclosure bounded by a perimeter wall – and in the middle a square keep. Here chance brought us into contact with a journalist, a young woman from Holland, who also knew about Rennes-le-Château. Such a contact might prove useful, so for a few days we all teamed up.

Next we headed back from Arques then up the climb to the ruins of the castle at Coustaussa. From here is a quite sublime view of the hilltop of Rennes-le-Château. The castle was built by the Trencavels in the mid-twelfth century, and was occupied by Simon de Montfort in 1210. This impressive ruin is close to the Paradise Pass, which leads from Couiza into the Corbières wine country. One tiny detail I can't overstate is the regard I have always had for the lives lived and the type of defence these fortresses afforded, when sources of water, and access to it, must have been a permanent problem. Under siege, often for months at a time, how could a community of Cathars survive (given that the digging of wells often requires depths of several hundred metres)?

We returned to Rennes-le-Château and took a stroll round the gardens, which were now open. The place attracts all sorts, and here we met a diviner (not of water, but of energy). I don't think he knew our secret. Unconcerned, I continued to admire the views. We visited the church, place crammed with eccentricities. Also the churchyard, cemetery, and Saunière's Tour Magdala, whose siting conforms to those alignments so conscientiously uncovered by Henry Lincoln – a hint in fact at the importance of everything in terms of spatial position. Saunière, whose church structure preceded him by seven or eight hundred years, had no power to change what had already been orientated – yet he could leave clues as to the meaning of those orientations (the very essence of Rennes-le-Château).

We looked more carefully at the gardens in the layout of their paths. We walked up to the Tour Magdala and climbed to the top. I noticed an innocent-looking roof ladder set out flat on the stone seats. I recalled Yeats's poem 'The Tower', from his collection of the same name:

Never had I more
Excited, passionate, fantastical
Imagination, nor an ear and eye
That more expected the impossible –

The ladder is a symbol of heavenward ascent.

From the terrace, with the trees in leaf, a view of the east was limited. Here I remind you of Saunière's Jerusalem model, where eastward is the Mount of Olives, and also Bethany, the village where Jesus's friends Martha, Mary and Lazarus lived. At the porch entrance to Saunière's villa Bethania, I noticed that many of the coloured panes of glass had slipped from their lead frames. Inside the villa, but close to his 'Hebrew' Temple there were some curious paintings – one of which depicted Christ with his heart exposed, but still apparently functioning. This meant nothing to me, but perhaps did mean something to the priesthood.

Outside were café chairs and tables, in the shade of the trees, all calm and quiet. After coffee and baguettes, we went to examine the water tower, which is south of the car park. I am not sure if it was still used to collect water, though its adorning sundial was still intact and prominent. So too was a ladder built into the tower, whose bottom rung was about three metres above the ground. Views to the south, west and east were stupendous.

I looked at the Tour Magdala. I followed the sweep of the path east past the entrance to the gardens. I saw all too clearly the similarity of line east from David's Tower in Jerusalem out to the Mount of Olives.

§

My very last visit to Rennes-le-Château was with my partner Jane. We spent a few days visiting the Sals valley and followed its small river up to the old agricultural village of Sougraigne, passing through Rennes-les-Bains. Over time the river had cut caves into the rock face, and approaching it at one such place, called the Fontaine des Amours, we could see the different elevations up and downstream. Here there were trout in the clear water, and adjacent to a buttress of rock, where we could see the remains of what looked like a mill, the water formed as a pool with a lip, over which it gently flowed. We wondered why such a building had been located here, as the village, about one and a half kilometres upstream, had a mill of its own. Curiously, there was an almost complete absence of vegetation on either side of the river bed.

We called into the Logis Ecluse au Soleil, with its terrace and swimming pool, and booked our evening meal. When we finally sat down to dinner, watching the late sun slide away over the hills of Rennes-le-Château, the proprietor proudly told us that a group of locals had had success producing pure salt from the river Sals, just as in years past. That confirmed that the Sals (apart from its name) was indeed salty, and explained why there was no vegetation immediately by it. We decided to explore its source the following day, which turned out to be almost unbearably hot. It saw us, at about 11.30, beginning our hike into the hills, equipped with water bottles, and having parked the car in a shady spot off the D74, just past Les Clamencis. The track was rough sandstone edged with birches and field maples, with plant life clinging for survival in the various cracks and crevices. At a later stage the track was in part overlapped by macadam, especially round the bends. Permanently in the air was the shrill of cicadas and the tinkle of cow and sheep bells as they roamed through the tree cover.

Where the stream was breaking over rocks and through the grassy tufts it was Jane who pointed to the presence of sea holly, which again was indicative of salt in the region (and which really got me thinking). Finally we reached an old farmhouse, and from here it was a short way through the thickets to the source of the river, beneath the rocky, tree-covered cliffs of the Rambosc la Verrerie. Here there was a white crust over the grass, and a strong smell of salt in the air. We picked out a few sample rocks and tasted the salt in them. Also the water here was very like seawater, which must have meant a large deposit of rock salt nearby. There was a clear and direct view, looking back the way we had come, of Rennes-le-Château – way down in the valley. I mused to myself that if Rennes-le-Château sat on a salt mine, what better place was there than this for those whose livelihood it was, who would naturally wish to protect their resource! Certainly nearby were some old guard houses, now in ruins, and there were also the ruins of salt pits farther down towards the car, marked on the map as Les Salines.

We headed back to the car and for another dinner at Sougraigne, where this time we sat watching kites wheeling across the twilit sky. When we spoke to the chef we were told, almost jokingly, as salt entered the conversation, that when Hannibal crossed the Alps it was for precisely the purpose of acquiring that substance, which in those days was as valuable as gold. The next day, when we explored the countryside again, we actively sought out plant life whose dependency was salt. Some we found on the old stone path to the rear of the castle at Rennes-le-Château, while vegetation on the north side of the hill tended to be sparse and poor, with perhaps these areas either deficient in nutrients or over-supplied with salt. After that we found more sea holly, which grows only in salty places.

When Saunière built his highway, the underlying motive may have been to divert attention from the north side of the hill. Re-channelling the old water course or culvert – while on the face of it providing pumped fresh water from Couiza to the people of Rennes-le-Château – could well have been a convenient distraction, had he been attempting to put a brine works into operation. In northern Europe, solution mining and brine evaporation is the most common process for the production of industrial and edible salt. From above ground water is pumped into the subterranean rock salt deposits, to produce fully saturated brine, which is then pumped back to the surface. Originally, salt production involved boiling the brine in open pans, so leaving salt crystals once the water had evaporated (though nowadays is done in huge evaporator vessels under vacuum).

The church at Rennes-le-Château, when of Arian denomination, was then only a chapel inside the castle, so that the people of the village worshipped not there but at the church of St Peter (this has long disappeared, but was situated slightly more to the south). When I looked in and around some of the old houses near the church, I found in an open shed a huge chunk of hewn sandstone. In it was an area of indentation, shallow at the bottom and rising to an edge, and looking very much like an early salt pan. In part it was stained white. I found also in the *reposoir des morts*, which is situated in the churchyard, the remains of an old metal pump. On the outside of the north wall was a drain or water collector, and a pipe from it led to the old underground cistern. Flash photos I had previously taken inside this cistern showed a dark tide mark, about a metre high. One side was crazed, and the other was whitish in colour.

In the cemetery, valerian grows close to Saunière's grave, a plant that in medicine is used as a sedative (and incidentally in symbolic terms is associated with the planet Mercury). Inside the church the tiles in the chancel, close to the altar, are patterned with small white cubes – possibly cubes of salt.

The Dead Sea is east of Jerusalem, so on the basis that Rennes-le-Château is modelled on that city, the salt mine we're looking for I assume is in a similar orientation. It was this I think that Saunière discovered, underneath Rennes-le-Château on its eastern and northern sides, and it was that that either directly or indirectly gave Saunière his wealth. Salt was known as 'white gold', and from the Middle Ages onward the quantity of salt mined and its market price were set by the archbishops of Salzburg (literally, 'salt castle'), who also regulated its trade and transport. Saunière's mine, even if long since disused for salt-production purposes, would nevertheless be a natural repository for all sorts of valuable artefacts, and was very probably used over a span of centuries as a clearing house for treasures, coins, documents, religious relics, etc. If among all that booty Saunière discovered seals or documents of great political importance, at a point in history when the internal map of Europe was about to be redrawn, then that in itself might lead him to do business with the Habsburgs, whose own power and influence were dwindling.

Salt provided the economic conditions for art and culture to flourish, and was a commodity the Cathars had in abundance (and which the Pope didn't). Salt was also highly prized for its medicinal properties. Salt will also have played its part in the study and pursuit of alchemy, with perhaps the famous Arab alchemist, Rhazes, having his name perpetuated in the very region of Rennes-le-Château, the Razès. Perhaps at one point it was the Knights Templar who controlled and regulated the salt trade, from the Dead Sea back into Europe, with castles such as the Château de Templiers acting as protectorates, in the flow of revenue, back and forth and en route to Rennes-le-Château.

16 Closing steps

I am, then, strongly inclined to think of Saunière's Rennes-le-Château, in the layout of its paths, gardens and walls, as modelled on the Jerusalem of the Crusader period (1099-1187 CE), which like Jerusalem is perched on a hilltop. As we have seen, my point of first reference – or two points superposed – is David's Tower, Jerusalem, the home of Jerusalem's governor, or Saunière's Tour Magdala. Commencing here, we can work round in a clockwise motion, due north to Patriarch Street, east to the Church of the Holy Sepulchre, on to St Stephen's Gate (or Saunière's greenhouse) and the Palace of la Latine. The Palace of la Latine corresponds to the kitchen in Rennes-le-Château. South along Malcuisinat Street brings us into Covered Street. From here we can return to David's Tower, or the Tour Magdala, by turning into David Street – or we could go east into Temple Street. From there we can take a route north called the Street of the Furriers, which leads us into Spanish Street. Spanish Street takes us back to the kitchen or Palace of la Latine. Returning along the Street of the Furriers brings us to baths in Jerusalem or a reservoir in Saunière's duplicate. This is a point close either to the Temple Mount or the church of Rennes-le-Château.

Jerusalem's Dome of the Rock was built in the first Muslim period (640-1099 CE), and just north of this is the Monastery of the Temple, a Franciscan building. The church in Rennes-le-Château occupies the same relative map co-ordinate as the monastery – both church and monastery lie in an east-west direction – a detail that had prompted me to recall the inscription Saunière had carved in Latin over his church door, in its echo of Thomas à Kempis. That in turn has led me to ask: did entry here parallel entry to a monastery, or a monastic order, or retirement from the world?

The Dome of the Rock is an octagonal building situated on the

Temple Mount, and is the oldest complete example of early Muslim architecture still surviving. It was not intended as a place of worship. It was a shrine to protect the Foundation Stone – the rock where, as tradition has it, Abraham prepared his son Isaac for sacrifice, and which was, in the first and second Temple periods, the site of the Holy of Holies. It was built in the seventh century. During the Crusader period, which succeeded the first Muslim period, the Temple Mount became a religious centre and the Dome of the Rock was renamed Templum Domini – Temple of the Lord.

To the Muslims, in that first period, the entire Temple Mount was known as El Aqsa, which in Arabic means 'the distant place'. The El Aqsa Mosque was built here in 715 CE. It was destroyed by an earthquake in 746, and was rebuilt in 780. In 985 it was destroyed again. With the arrival of the crusaders it became a church, and also the headquarters of the Templars. The Templars called it the Temple of Solomon. Since the octagonal outer structure of the Dome of the Rock lies just north of this, this might explain why the Knights Templar erected so many buildings or churches with eight sides (eight in numerology the number of paradise regained. Also usually the Christian font is octagonal, and there are eight beatitudes).

Now no one, so far as I know, has made these comparisons – a ground map of Jerusalem alongside that of Rennes-le-Château – with its obvious coincidence of pathways and landmarks. A possible reason for this is the many other discoveries concerning Rennes-le-Château, and the conjecture they have naturally resulted in, all serving to obscure or leave overlooked some of the simpler details. This is not to mention the many new age ideas clouding our topic.

Saunière represented the Templum Domini in his church garden by a ring of brickwork on which his Calvary is situated. If you take a bearing in Jerusalem – albeit from the printed map – from David's Tower to the northern limit of the Templum Domini, you get an angle of approximately twenty-three and a half degrees with the horizontal – which may simply be coincidence. (Though an interesting observation here is that the Hebrew word for tower is migdal, which bears obvious similarities with the word Magdala. South of the Tour Magdala is an area not unlike that south of the towers of Herod's palace, which itself was just below the citadel and David's Tower.)

Less coincidental is the angle the 'blue apples' clue drew my attention to. In Chapter 12 I showed how a midday beam of light passes through a stained glass window on the church's south side in its composition of those blue apples. The window in question bears a depiction of the raising of Lazarus, and is set into its stone frame at an angle of forty-one degrees. This is the same angle, you will recall, as the angle between the sun and Venus for the 1780 winter solstice. (See Figure 3.) This set me thinking.

I now did what many of my predecessors have done – notably Henry Lincoln – and began to consider the first parchment (see Figure 6) as not only a cipher, but perhaps also a diagram able to render geometric patterns. Henry Lincoln certainly discovered that when some of its specific textual figures are connected by pencil lines, which you draw with the aid of a ruler, an arrangement of triangles eventually gives shape to a five-pointed star. What Lincoln goes on to uncover is complex models of geometry all linked through carved, textual, and topographic information – a discovery the validity of which I wouldn't wish to challenge.

I would just say however that it is possible to derive other information from some of the co-ordinates that Lincoln himself uses. In the top left-hand corner of the parchment is a curious triangular symbol that forms part of his pentacle, but to me is very reminiscent of an astronomer's quadrant (see Figure 7). After a great deal of experimentation, I have finally seen a correspondence between the diagram it is possible to arrive at from the layout of the parchment and our figure for the winter solstice for 1780 (Figure 3). If my hypothesis is correct (and for me there is too much evidence to suggest that it isn't) then a symbolic association with Venus that we are supposed to identify on the ground becomes possible. Here is the procedure I followed, working on parchment one:

1. First consider that triangle at the top of the manuscript, which I have likened to a quadrant (see Figure 8). Extend the two outer sides of its triangle as far as they will go. It will be noticed that the upper of these two lines intersects the + symbol at line four.

2. A line drawn from the upper vertex of the triangle to the + symbol in line

ten will be seen to be at an angle of twenty-three and a half degrees to the lower of the lines we extended in 1).

3. A line drawn vertically down also from the + symbol in line ten similarly meets the lower of the two lines we extended in 1) at twenty-three and a half degrees.

4. A vertical line drawn up from the + symbol in line seven also produces an angle of twenty-three and a half degrees. It therefore doesn't seem unreasonable to draw a vertical line through the only other remaining + symbol, which is at line four. This can be extended through that PS inscription enclosed by a broken ellipse.

5. The triangle this so far gives us bears a remarkable resemblance to the small triangle in our diagram of the 1780 winter solstice (see Figure 3), with the sun at the lowest vertex, the equator at the middle vertex, and the north-south line touching the upper vertex.

6. From this I deduce that the geometry associated with the parchment is intended as a representation of the 1780 winter solstice, and furthermore is a figure we are supposed to replicate somewhere on the ground at Rennes-le-Château.

7. Now, we know that the 'blue apples' window is set in its casement at forty-one degrees, so if we now envisage the figure we have so far drawn as somewhere on the ground south of that window, and we draw a forty-one-degree line through the apex of our quadrant-like triangle corresponding to that of the winter solstice diagram, we see this intersect the last vertical we drew (through the + symbol in line four). (See Figure 9.) That point, I believe, is the point on the ground we are being asked to identify as Venus, which completes the correspondences between the two figures. This is borne out by other data for the 1780 winter solstice, which shows the right ascension of the sun to Venus as eighteen degrees. A line drawn at eighteen degrees on our parchment diagram from the sun does indeed intersect that point corresponding with Venus.

If we now consider all this information in terms of our previous unravelling of the second parchment clue, we can I think make further deductions. You will recall from Chapter 12 that the clue reading

> by the cross of this horse of God I complete this demon guardian at midday blue apples

I translated to

> by the Calvary of the sun I fix Venus at midday blue apples

If at midday we are standing to the south of the church, then the sun is behind us. If we stand somewhere on the vertical line our Figures 8 and 9 show projecting from the sun, then by the Calvary I think is intended to show the exact point at which we stand. This means that the church window is about four metres in front of us, and it is from this measure that we can arrive at a scale for a reconstruction on the ground of our final representation shown in Figure 9. I fix Venus means that we locate that point on the ground as the entrance to the treasure's vault. This is in Saunière's grotto, and without myself having been there with surveying equipment (which I don't think I would have been allowed to do) my rough guess is that the area of the grotto is linked to either the *reposoir des morts* or the *ancienne urne baptismale* (see Figure 4). One of these I believe conceals an entrance to a part of Rennes-le-Château where there are enormous natural caves, including a salt mine, within which the treasures of Yahweh, or Jerusalem, the Holy Grail – or whatever Saunière found – are awaiting rediscovery.

I can offer up my shovel, and only appeal to the French authorities that my own is the first incision in the ground, since it's a well known fact that the civil code prohibits anyone in France, other than an archaeologist, from carrying out an excavation.

Afterword

The calculations I set out in the last chapter represent a much simplified version of all the correspondences I discovered, and which I continue to discover, in the layout of parchment one – a web and a mesh of detail all too mind-boggling for the scope of a succinct little book such as this. Perhaps in a separate pamphlet I shall one day elaborate this remarkable phenomenon in something like its fullness, but for the moment shall confine myself only to passing reference to what seem to me the most striking adjuncts. For example, it is possible to plot a centre and radius on to the parchment geometry, and having done so draw an arc that corresponds with the equator in the winter solstice figure. It is possible also to overlay this same parchment geometry onto a scaled down reproduction of Poussin's *Shepherds of Arcadia*, wherein the twenty-three-and-a-half-degree line, which we extended from that curious figure that looks like a quadrant, coincides with the shepherd's staff that is also inclined at twenty-three and a half degrees – a detail that first got me thinking about the winter solstice. Once that correspondence has been made, others follow – particularly the position of Venus (which seems to be synchronised in both the parchment and the painting).

I might add also that in the Teniers painting (Figure 10) the two staffs are crossed at an angle of about $117^3/_4$ degrees on one side and about $62^1/_4$ degrees on the other. The angle sixty-two and a quarter degrees is the sum of twenty-three and a half degrees and thirty-eight and three-quarter degrees. As we have seen, twenty-three and a half degrees is the angle of the sun to the earth on the day of the winter solstice – but according to the spherical triangle, which also belongs to our solstice diagram, and which in fact is shown (see Figure 3), thirty-eight and three-quarter degrees approximates to the thirty-nine-degree angle separating the sun and Venus. I don't know whether these are just coincidences, or whether they are there among the details to tell us that we're looking for the right things.

As we know, Saunière left useful pointers close to his church, to show his successors that in dealing with the encryptions not all of it is necessarily a matter of textual interpretation. We have already seen the significance of the Calvary, but one issue I haven't taken up, which *is* a matter of textual interpretation, is the inscription that appears on a part of it – CHRISTUS AOMPS DEFENDIT. According to Lincoln and friends the AOMPS probably stands for Antiquus Ordo Mysticusque Prioratus Sionis, but I would like to offer an alternative to that – being, Arc Ours Méridien Polaris, or Polaris's meridian arc from the bear (the Pole Star is in the Little Bear, or Ursa Minor Constellation). This is no more an abbreviated mix of French and Latin than has been found in other clues.

One further nicety that I think Saunière arranged lies in the fact that a perpendicular drawn from the forty-one-degree window into the interior of his church strikes the north wall at the niche of Saint-Antoine-Ermite – St Anthony the hermit, one subject of the Teniers painting. I do not overlook either Sauniere's fondness for puns, both language and visual, one of his most perfect representations of both being the cross in his church garden. The north side bears the inscription 'Christus Regnat In Cruce Salus', the south side 'Christus Imperat In Cruce Vita', the west 'Christus Vincit', and the east 'Aimons Saluons Respectons Notre Croix' – north and east having 'sal' in common, salt, an industry we have already discussed.

At this point I might as well add too, at the risk of jumping on the new age van, that I have often conjectured to myself as to the derivation of the enormous wealth that the Knights Templar came to possess. I do not at times find it difficult to believe that theirs was a secret knowledge, ranging over the mechanics and architectonics of building construction, to devices for generating electricity and, hermetically speaking, making water – assets more valuable than gold, more valuable even than salt. This may seem fanciful, but is it absolutely beyond the bounds of possibility that certain scientific or technological techniques have been lost on a succeeding age? I have pondered – and alluded to this in the text above – on the ability of the Cathars to sustain themselves under siege for extended periods, when access to water might have been at best extremely uncertain. This is just a thought, but had they a method, or a formula, then who really knows? Perhaps they built their castles over salt pits. Or perhaps this is one hypothesis just too far, or perhaps is a secret only for the chosen, for the remnant, for Yahweh's elect – Yahweh who lies there dormant, in suspension, inanimate, so to say at temporal degree zero.

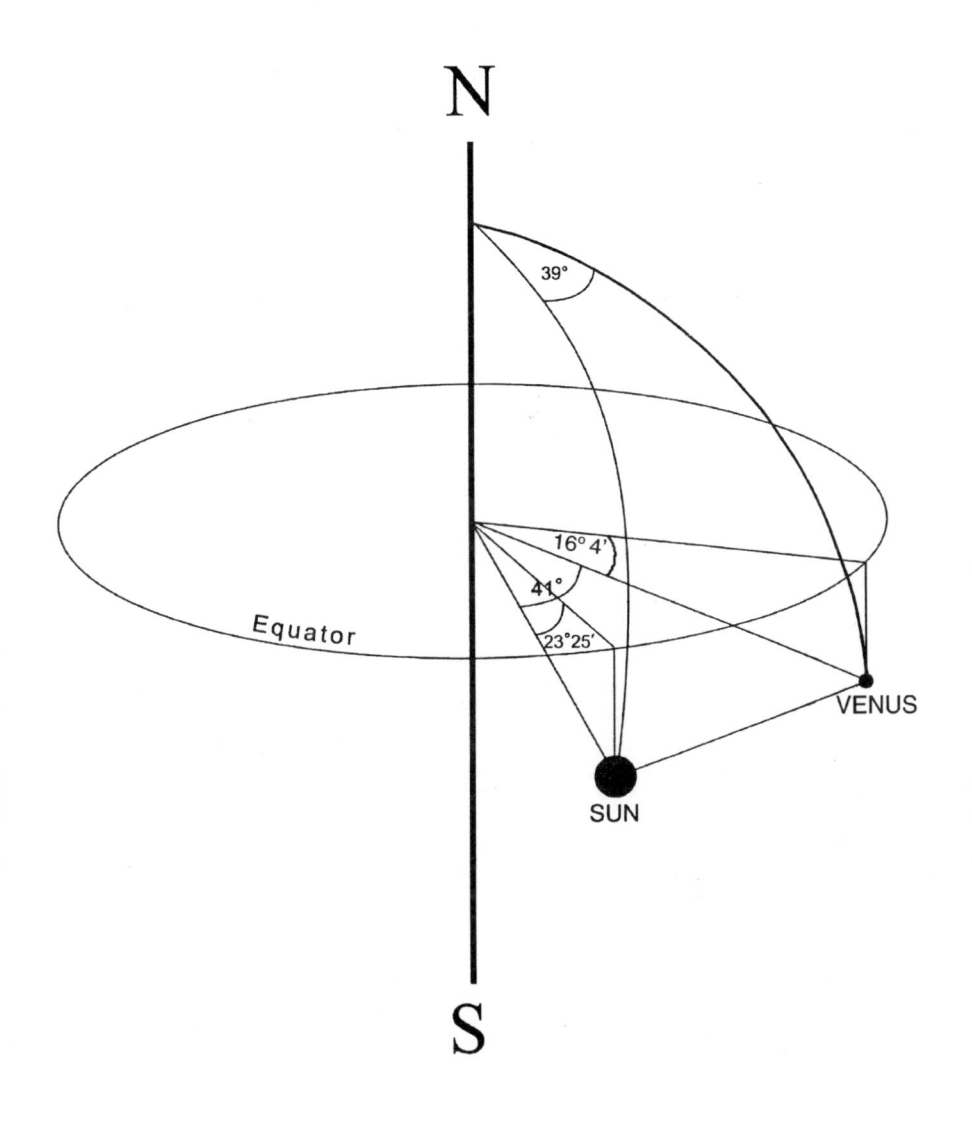

Figure 3.
The difference between Plane and Spherical Angles.
1780 Winter Solstice.

Figure 4.
Rennes-le-Château —
Plan and Visitors' Guide and details of the Cathar Circuit.

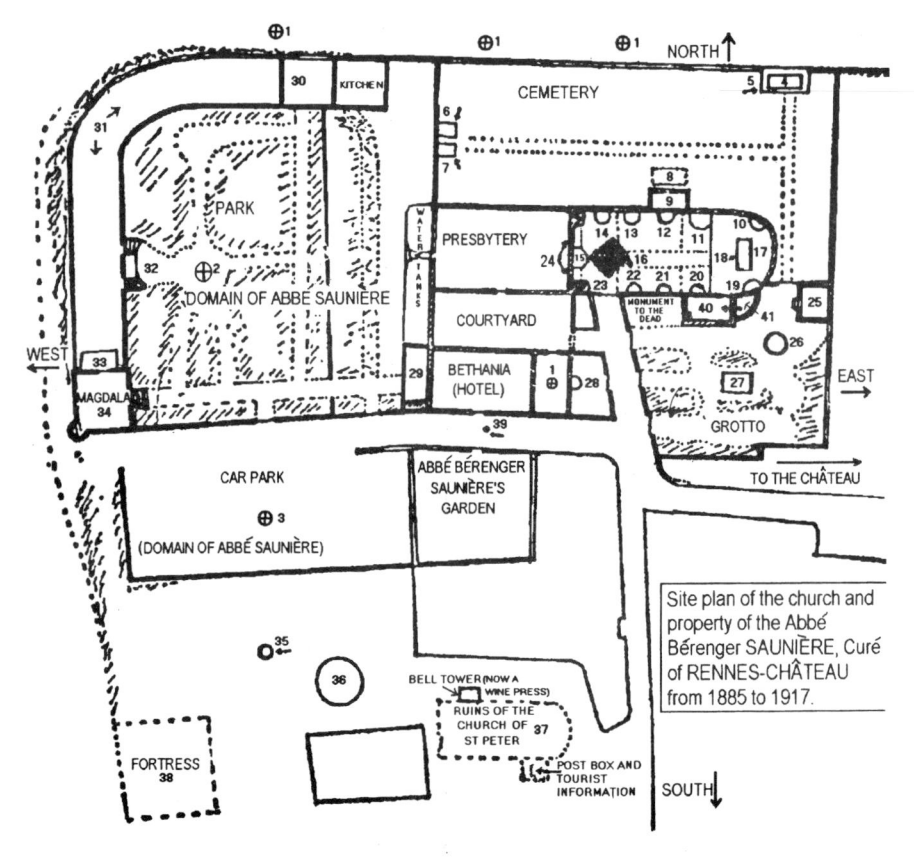

Fig. 3.4. Rennes-le-Château - Church and Domain.
RENNES-LE-CHÂTEAU. List of places:
1. Excavations made in 1964.
2. Excavations to 18 metres.
3. Excavations to 17 metres.
4. Stone defaced by Bérenger Saunière.
5. Ossuary.
6. Tomb of Abbé Bérenger Saunière.
7. Tomb of Marie Denarnaud.

8. Tomb of Hautpoul-Blanchefort Ladies.
9. Bell tower.
10. Saint Joseph.
11. Throne.
12. Saint Anthony the Hermit.
13. Saint Germaine.
14. Saint John the Baptist.
15. Confessional.
16. Chess board.
17. Altar.
18. Mary Magdalene tableau.
19. The Virgin Mary.
20. Saint Anthony of Padua.
21. Saint Mary Magdalene.
22. Saint Roch.
23. The devil Asmodeus.
24. Large tableau.
25. Repository for the dead.
26. Ancient baptismal urn.
27. Calvary.
28. Our Lady of Lourdes.
29. Chapel of Abbé Bérenger Saunière.
30. Orangery.
31. Terrace or belvedere.
32. Staircase and pond.
33. Veranda.
34. Magdala tower.
35. Ancient pits (blocked up).
36. Water tower.
37. Ruins of Saint Peter's Church.
38. Site of fortress.
39. Ancient pits (blocked up).
40. Sacristy.
41. Small secret room.

Copyright — Tatiana Kletzky – Pradere (1983).

Figure 5.
Map of Jerusalem in the Crusader Period
(1099 – 1187).

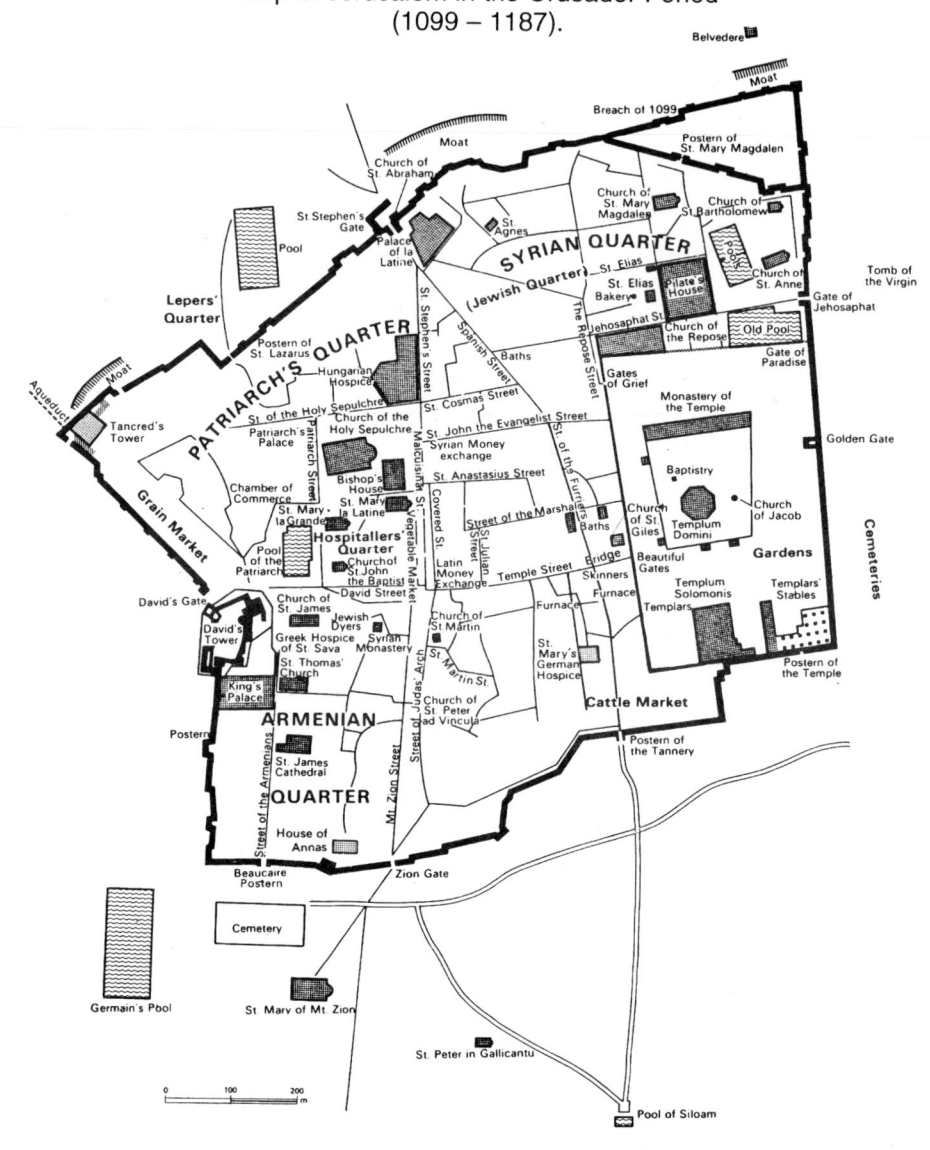

Copyright: Carta, Jerusalem.

Figure 6.

1st MANUSCRIPT

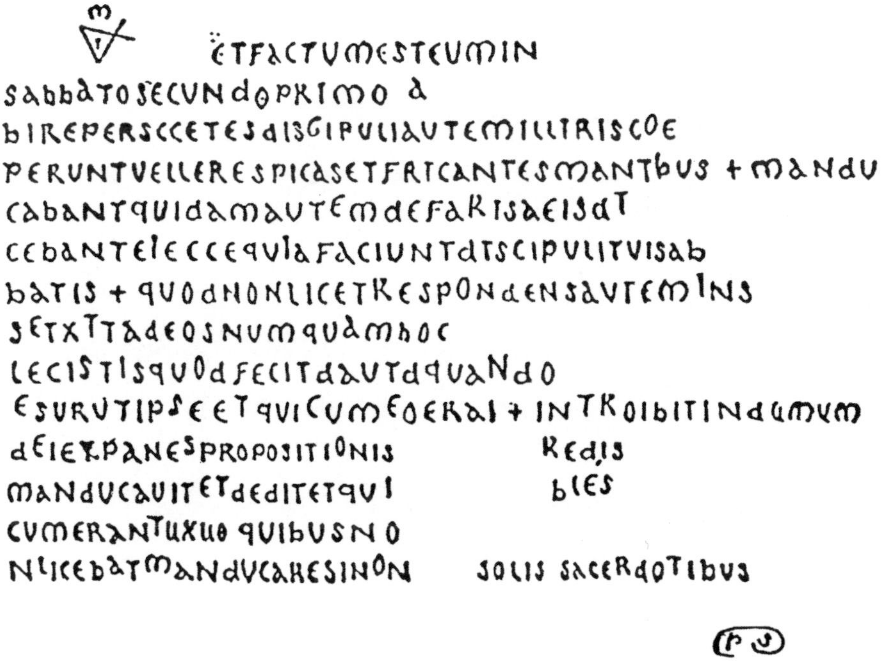

͞ETFACTUMESTCUMIN
SabbatoSecundoprimo a
bireperscceTesdiscipuliautemillirisCoe
peruntvelleresPicasetfricantesmanTbus + mandu
cabantquidamautemdefaRisaeisat
cebanteieCCequiafaciuntdtscipulitvisab
batis + quodnonliceTRespondensautemins
setxTTadeosnumquamhoc
LecistisquodfecitdautdquaNdo
esurutipseetquicumfoerai + introibitindumum
dei et panesProPositionis   Redis
manducauit et deditetqui   bies
cumerantuxuo quibusno
nlicebatmanducaResinon   solis sacerdotibus

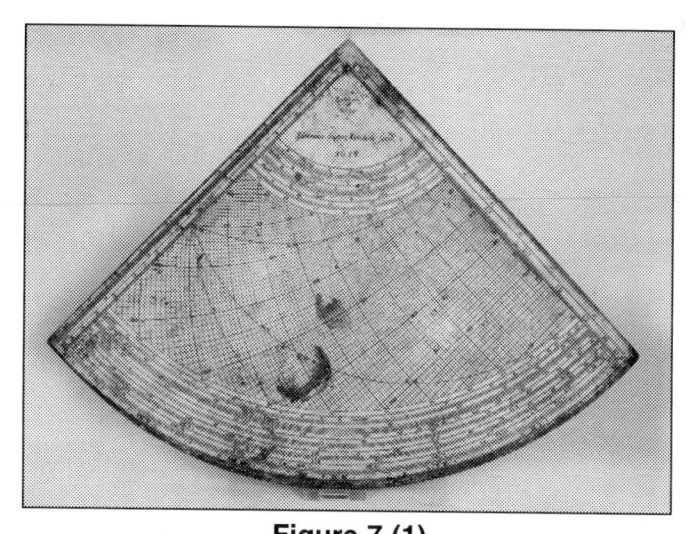

Figure 7 (1).
A Paper Horary Quadrant by Henry Sutton, 1658,
radius 277 m.m., pasted on wood.
Whipple Museum of the History of Science, Cambridge University.

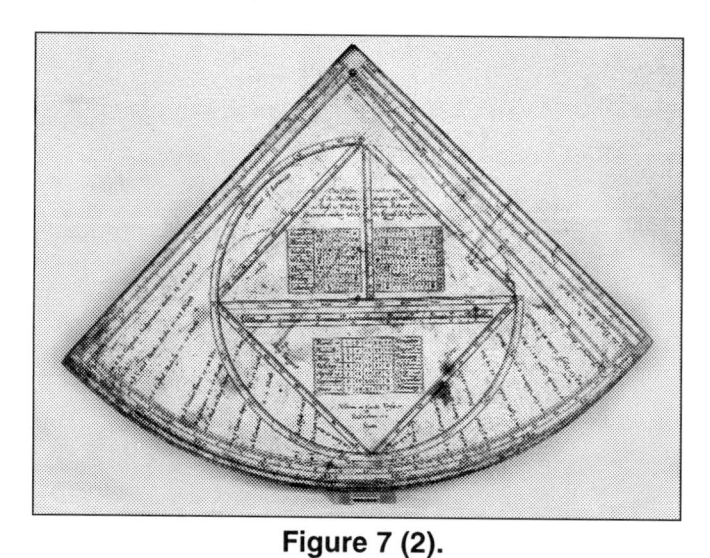

Figure 7 (2).
A Paper Horary Quadrant by Henry Sutton, 1658,
radius 277 m.m., pasted on wood.
Whipple Museum of the History of Science, Cambridge University.

Figure 8.

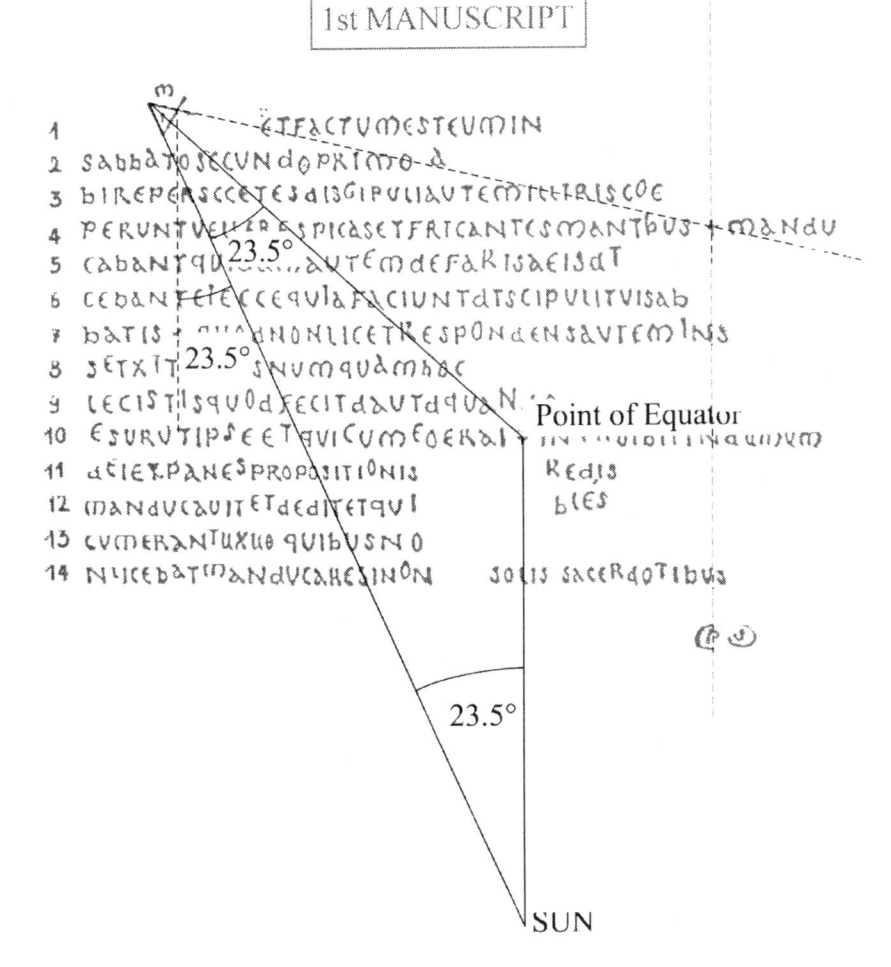

1st MANUSCRIPT

1 ETFACTUMESTEUMIN
2 SAbbATOSECUNdOPRIMO A
3 bIREPERSCCETES dISGIPULIAUTEMTHERISCOE
4 PERUNTUELIERASPICASETFRICANTESMANTbUS + MANdU
5 CAbANTqU...AUTEMdEFARISAEISdT
6 CEdANFETECCEqUIAFACIUNTdTSCIPULITVISAb
7 bATIS   NONLICETRESPONdENSAUTEMINS
8 SETXIT SNUMqUAMhAC
9 LECISTISqUOd FECITdAUTdqUA N Point of Equator
10 ESURUTIPSEETTqVICUMFOERAT
11 ATIETPANESPROPOSITIONIS   Redis
12 MANdUCAUITETdEdITETqUI   bIES
13 CUMERANTUXU QUIbUSNO
14 NUCEbATMANdUCAREINON   SOLIS SACERdOTIbUS

23.5°

SUN

Winter Solstice.

101

Figure 9.

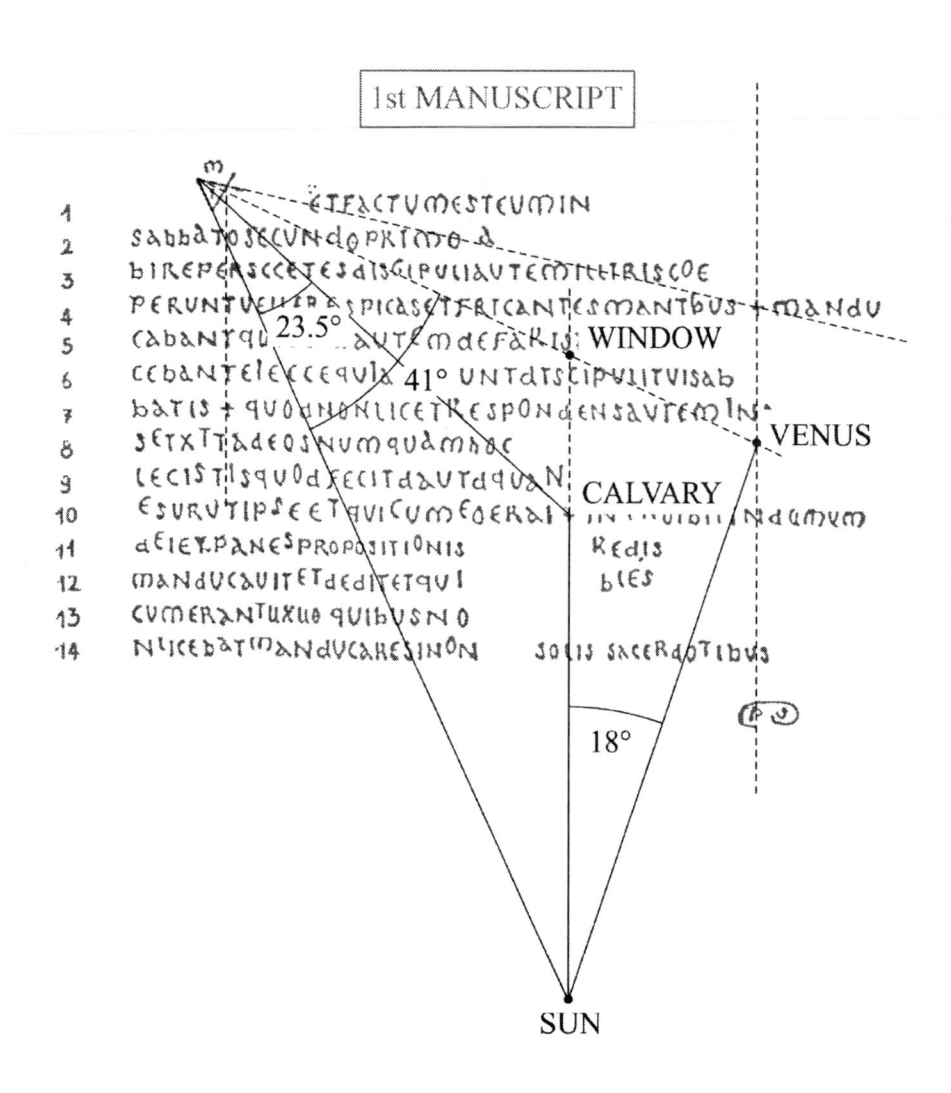

Winter Solstice with Venus.

Figure 10

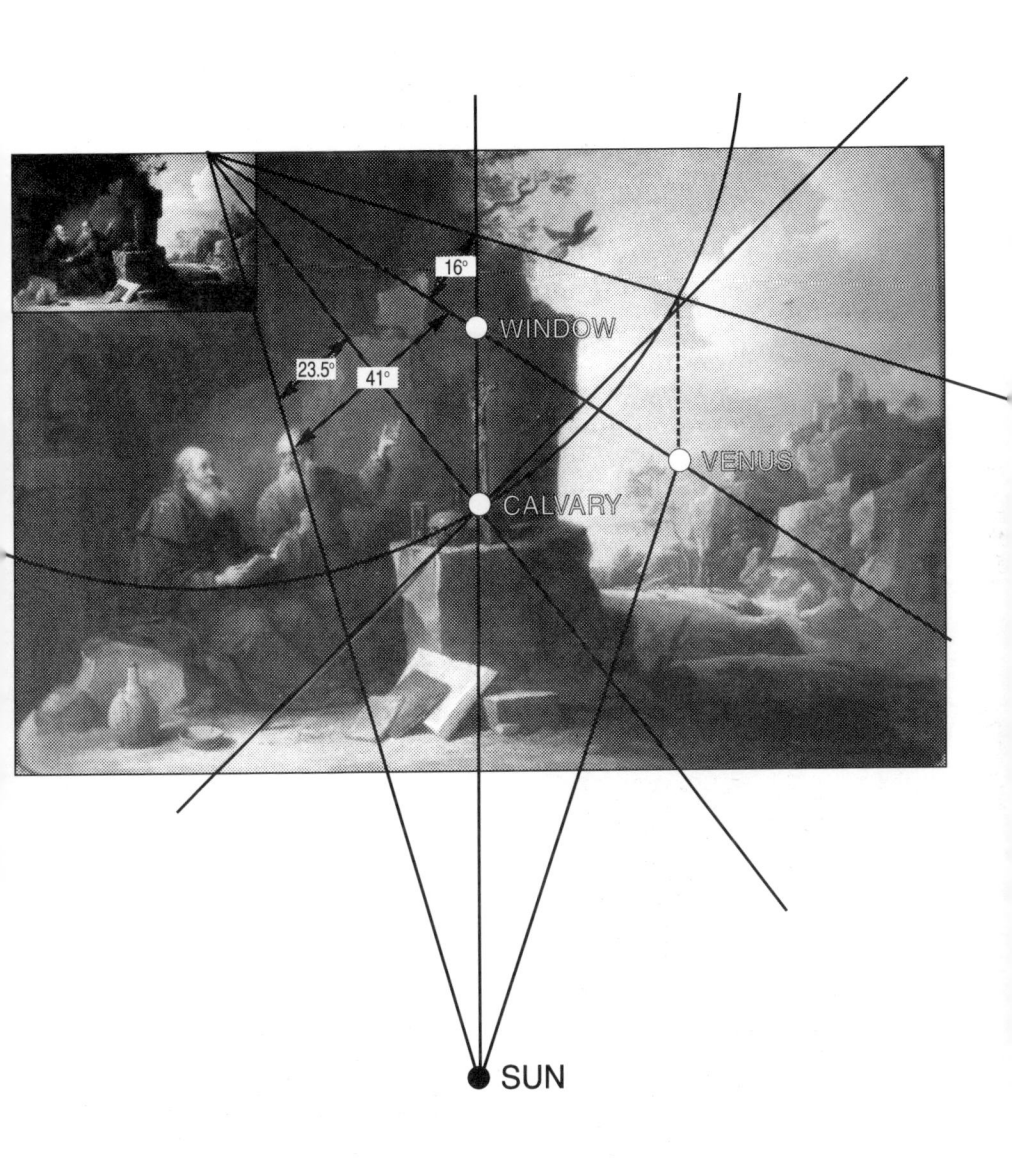

St. Antony and St. Paul,
by David Teniers the Younger.

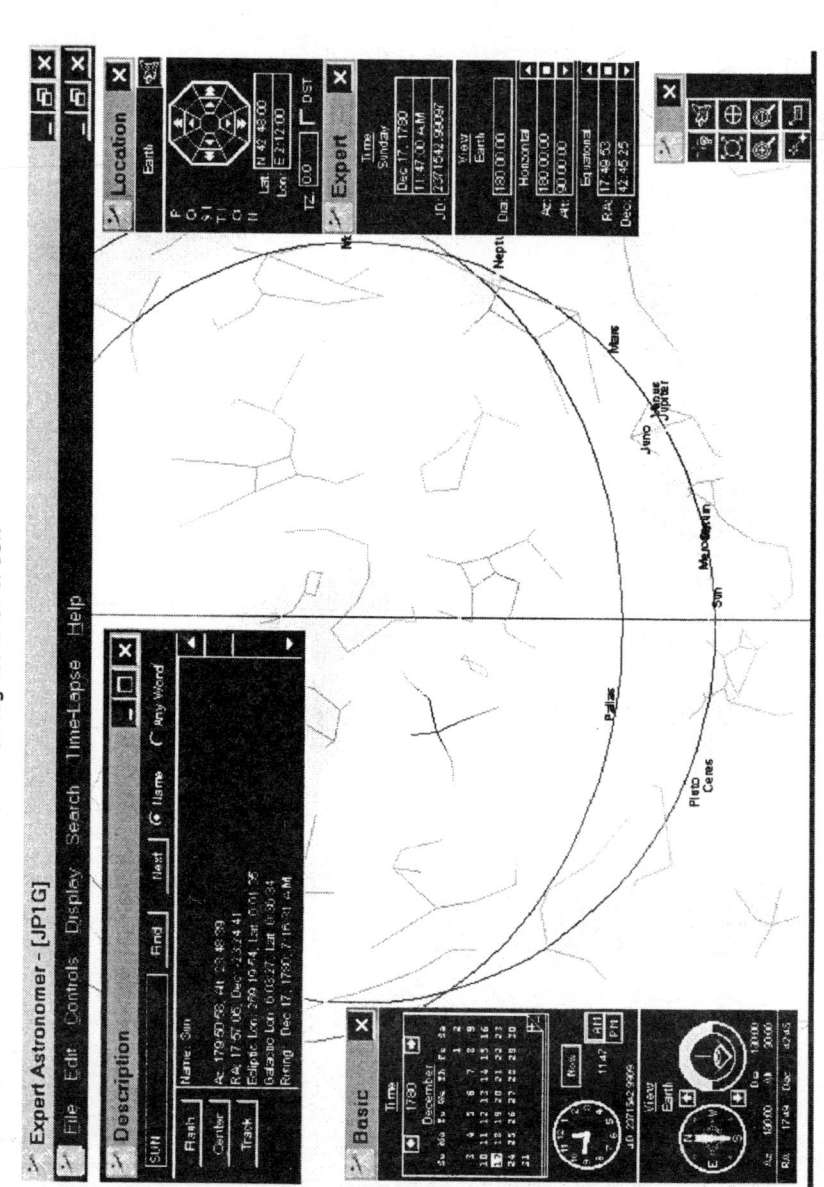

17 Dec 1780   Local time 1147am   VENUS 39.69 degrees EAST of SUN

Figure 11.

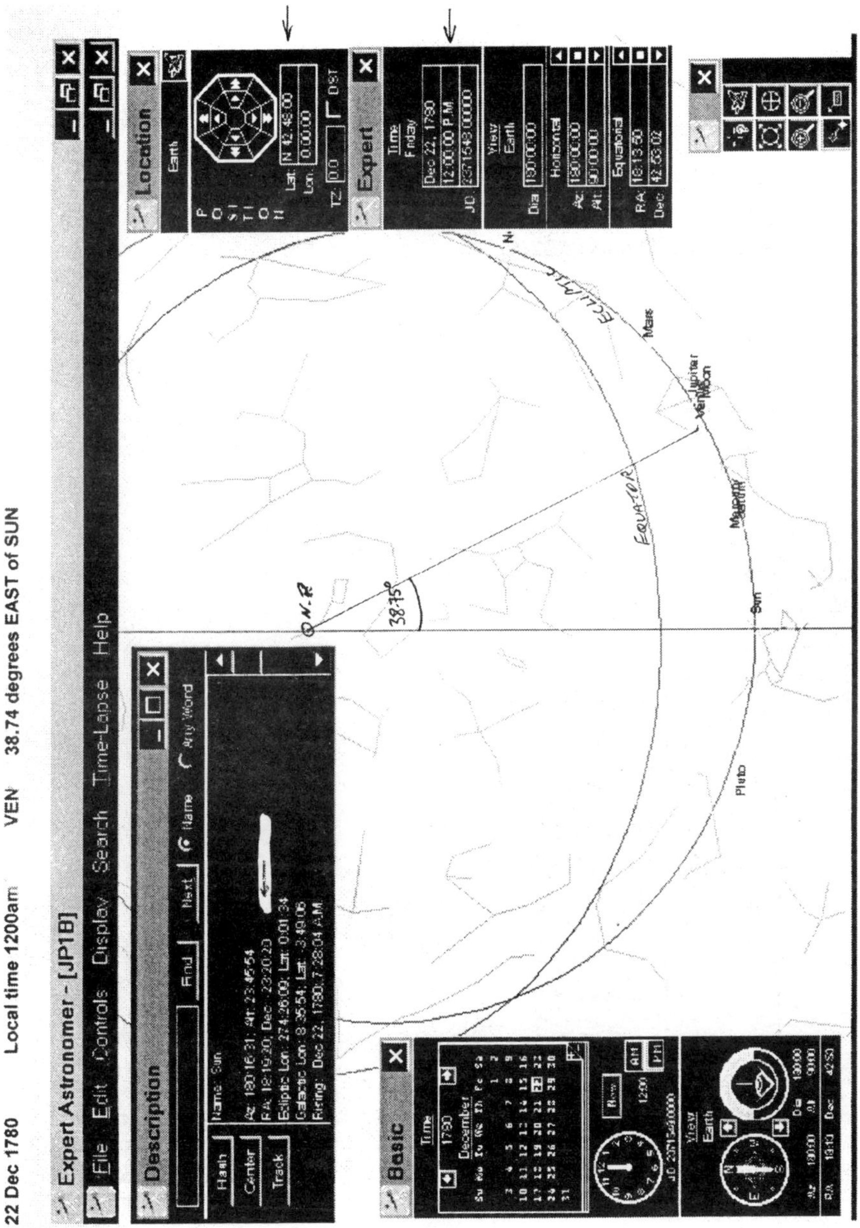
22 Dec 1780
Local time 1200am
VEN
38.74 degrees EAST of SUN
Expert Astronomer - [JP1B]
File Edit Controls Display Search Time-Lapse Help
Description
Basic
Location
Expert
ECLIPTIC
EQUATOR
38.75°
N.P
Mars
Jupiter
Moon
Venus
Mercury
Saturn
Sun
Pluto

Figure 12.

2nd MANUSCRIPT

JESVSCVRGOANTCCSCXATYESPASCSHACVENJTTLETHQANIAMVRAT
JVCKAOTIAZA-VVSMORTYOVSQVCMMSVSCTYTAVITIYESVSFEACERVNT
.LAVICM·TTCAENAPMTLTETOMARTHAHMINISTRRALITHASARVSO
VEROVNXVSFRATTE·AISLOUMIENTATIVSCVJMMARTALERGOACHCEP
TTIKTHRAMYNNGENTTJNARATPFTSTICIQPRETIOVSTETVNEXT.TPE
APCSTERVAETCXTESRSTICAYPIIRTSNSVISPEPAESERTPTETAOMLESTM
YLFITAESTEEXVNGETNTTOAAEREAIXAITERGOVRNVMEXAGTSCIPVAL
TSETVIXTVAAXGCAHSORTISQVIYERATCVHMTRAATTTYHVSQTVAREHOGCVN
HEN VIVMNONXVENYITGRECENPATSAENAARVSETAATVMESGTE
GENTCSIAIXINVTEMHOECNONQVSTAAECGAENTSPERRTINELEAT
AACVTMSEAQVHMFVRELRTETLOVCVIOSHCAHENSECAQVACMVTIIEHA
NMTVRPOTRAHETEATXITEJRGOTESHVSSINEPTLLAMVNITXAITERMS
EPVLGTVKAEMSEAESERVNETILLQVAPAVPSERESENHIMSEMPGERHA
HEMTTSNOHLTISCVMFMEAVIETMNONSESMPERHAVLEUSCJOGNO
VILIEROTZVRHAMVQLIAEXTMVAACTSTQVTATLOLTCESTXETYENE
ARVNTNONNPROTEPRTESU·ETANT·MMSEAVILVZA RVMPVTAER
ZH·TQVEM KSVSCTAOVITAMORRTVTSCPOGITAVRERVNTAHVTEMP
RVTNCTPESSACERCAOTVMVMTETLAZCARVMTNATERFICTRENTY
LVTAMYLVTTPROPQTERILAXVMAHTHGNTCRVGT·AETSNCTCRCA
ACHANTINIESVM

NO☉ ↓IS

JESV. MEACLA. VVLNERUM ✚ SPES.VNA. PŒNITENTIVM.
PER. MAGAALENÆ. LACRYMAS ✚ PECCATA. NOSTRA. ATLVAS.

Figure 13.

Sources

Andrews, Richard, Schellenberger, Paul, *The Tomb of God* (London, 1999).
Bahat, Dan, *Carta's Historical Atlas of Jerusalem* (Jerusalem, 1976).
Baigent, Michael, Leigh, Richard, *The Dead Sea Scrolls Deception* (London, 1992).
Baigent, Michael, Leigh, Richard, Lincoln, Henry, *The Holy Blood and the Holy Grail* (London, 1982).
Borges, Jorge Luis (trans James E. Irby), 'Tlön, Uqbar, Orbis Tertius' in *Labyrinths* (Harmondsworth, 1986).
Burns, P. F., *First Steps in Astronomy* (London, nd).
Cooper, J. C., *An Illustrated Encyclopaedia of Traditional Symbols* (London, 1982).
Fanthorpe, Patricia and Lionel, *The Holy Grail Revealed* (North Hollywood, 1982).
Hebert, A. G., *The Throne of David* (London, 1942).
Lincoln, Henry, *The Holy Place* (London, 1991).
Mann, A. T., *The Round Art* (Cheltenham, 1979).
Moore, Patrick, *The Observer's Book of Astronomy* (London, 1965).
Norvill, Roy, *The Treasure Seeker's Treasury* (London, 1978).
Roberts, J. M., *A History of Europe* (New York, 1997).
Sède, Gérard de, *Signé: Rose Croix* (Librairie Plon, 1967).
Sobel, Dava, *Longitude* (London, 1998).
Wilson, Ian, *Jesus: The Evidence* (London, 1996).
Wright, Christopher, *Poussin Paintings* (London, 1984).

Château d'Arques, 1999

The Author puzzling over the clues
at Rennes-le-Château, August, 2001.